Praise for

CULTURIZE

"Every student doesn't need just one adult who is a champion for them; they need multiple adults. Casas doesn't just reaffirm that; he gives you multiple ways to make this happen from whatever position you are in. 'Average' is the new mediocre. Greatness is what we should strive for in every school, from every position. This book will be a tremendous push in that direction."

—**George Couros**, author, *The Innovator's Mindset*

"Jimmy knows school culture. And that's because he truly knows and cares about people. *Culturize* will give you the insights you need to champion for students, pursue excellence, and carry the banner for your school. There are so many great ideas here that I will use right away. I'm both challenged and inspired by what I've learned from Jimmy. I think you will be too. Your school culture is too important to miss out on reading this book."

—**David Geurin**, author, *Future Driven*, NASSP National Digital Principal, lead learner, Bolivar High School, Missouri

"Jimmy Casas is definitely willing to do whatever it takes. In *Culturize*, he draws on deep personal reasons for caring about the culture of school and the relationships that shape it. He provides tools, anecdotes, and the voices of other practitioners to hone in on students and the power and influence of adult relationships on the lives of the students we serve. His approach is powerful, and it guides readers to understand that school culture must be a daily focal point for all school leaders. I walked the experiences of his journey with him, and I learned some powerful lessons along the way. I see things differently now!"

—**Beverly Hutton**, Ed.D., deputy executive director, National Association of Secondary School Principals (NASSP)

"As a classroom teacher and education leader, *Culturize* resonated with me on multiple levels. I am constantly striving for my actions to reflect 'better than average' both inside and outside of my school. *Culturize* serves as a true compass north for anyone aiming to create a culture where outstanding leadership is the standard at all levels. Jimmy shares personal stories of his childhood as well as highlights of his vast experience as an educational leader on his journey to empower leaders. No matter your title or profession, page after page of this book will inspire you."

—**Kayla Delzer**, CEO, Top Dog Teaching Inc.,
author and globally awarded teacher

"For all those committed to improving student performance, *Culturize* is a must-read! The number one lesson learned through ongoing studies at The International Center for Leadership in Education of the nation's most rapidly improving schools reveal that 'culture trumps strategy.' The culture in these schools is anchored first and foremost on students, not simply on standards. School improvement begins by creating relationships. These relationships enable us to determine what is relevant to each student. Relevance then enables us to achieve academic rigor with our students. In *Culturize*, Jimmy Casas tells us how to set this in motion. It should be a handbook for all educators."

—**Dr. Bill Daggett**, founder and chairman,
International Center for Leadership in Education

"If you are a 'student' of school culture, this book must be on your shelf as a daily reference tool and reflection guide. Building school culture happens as a result of thoughtful, intentional, and reflective leadership. *Culturize* takes leaders on a reflective journey by using practical vignettes to illustrate solid approaches for building school culture in a variety of ways. This book is a must-read for those who are committed to building and sustaining a culture of excellence."

—**Sanee Bell**, Ed.D., principal, Morton Ranch Junior High

"Casas amps up the important conversations we all need to have on what it takes to establish and maintain an impactful school culture. *Culturize* provides a much-needed human-like perspective on the critical role leaders play on moving a school or district's culture from good to great. Casas does a phenomenal job of highlighting culture stories from various stakeholders' groups. Your mindset on culture in various educational settings will change in a positive way once you open this book."

—**Brad Currie**, 2017 NASSP National Assistant Principal of the Year, co-creator, #Satchat

"Jimmy Casas has directly impacted thousands of lives in the education community. He's done so through blogging, tweeting, presenting, and now, long-form writing. This book captures the essence that is Jimmy, and now all who read this will be as directly impacted as those whose lives he's touched through social media and in person."

—**Barry Saide**, director of curriculum and instruction, Tabernacle Township School District, Tabernacle, New Jersey

"Seth Godin taught me that 'you get the culture you deserve' as a leader. Ouch! That's quite a statement and an overwhelming idea, especially if your current culture stinks! Fortunately, in your hands is a book from a personal hero of mine, Jimmy Casas. Use this text as a playbook to build the culture of your dreams and the culture you deserve."

—**Danny "Sunshine" Bauer**, host, *Better Leaders Better Schools* podcast

"Jimmy does it again!! Jimmy shares personal stories, practical strategies, and most importantly, a direct challenge to the status quo. He asserts that average is not okay for our students, and he helps the reader understand how to move past whatever has become their status quo. This book is tremendous and will have a profound impact on its readers and the schools they serve."

—**Dr. P.J. Caposey**, superintendent, Meridian 223, author, *Making Evaluation Meaningful*

"Nothing can short circuit innovative ideas and practices in schools like a toxic culture. Creating the schools and experiences today's modern learners both need and deserve is difficult work, and it's up to leaders to bring these aspirations to fruition. In this book, Jimmy Casas leverages his long-time, award-winning leadership experience alongside dynamic and effective culture builders to challenge and inspire leaders to identify the average in their schools, move past the status quo, model the way, and lead and love with passion, purpose, and pride. Read this book to culturize your school and to live your excellence—every day."

—**Thomas C. Murray**, co-author, *Learning Transformed*, Director of Innovation, Future Ready Schools

"This book reads like a good conversation. A conversation that, while comfortable, is also compelling, affirming, reflective, challenging, and expectant. The messages in *Culturize* hit you directly in the space between your heart, your head, and your hands. What separates this book from others of a similar theme is how strengthening our culture is in the service of ensuring high levels of learning for all students and adults. Very few books succeed in being 'everything to everyone.' And while this is not what Jimmy sought to do, the fact is, this book is for ALL educators. In every chapter, I thought I had the target audience figured out. Is he speaking to school leaders? Teacher leaders? Instructional Coaches? Collaborative Teams? Support Professionals? The answer is YES. I found myself relating to one message that spoke to the classroom teacher in me. Another message spoke to me as a school leader. Most importantly, the book spoke to me as a champion for students. *Culturize* is a call to doing more of what works, a call to seeing the person behind every data point, and a call for educators to be fully awake and intentional about leveraging our power as influencers in the lives of the students we serve."

—**Kenneth C. Williams**, Unfold the Soul, Inc.

"*Culturize* is so much more than a book about how school leaders create strong culture in schools. It is a book written by someone who has 'walked the walk.' Through the illustrative examples of practice—his and others—Jimmy Casas paints the picture of a school leader's higher calling. School leaders there to work with adults and students as they go about the business of learning, but Casas urges us to look beyond the responsibility of leadership and focus on the "gift" of leadership. Those who work in schools know it is not an eight-hour-a-day job. (The hours are long and the work exhausting.) Casas implores us to embrace the work from a servant leader perspective and to focus on the fact that with every word and every action you are making a difference in the lives of the people with whom you work. The critical work of being a culture builder, as he describes it, is supported with ideas and examples of how to embrace becoming a culture leader in your school. Casas knows the work of the school leader is never finished, and throughout the book he poses thought-provoking self-reflection questions that cause the leader to become the learner. Great leaders are also great teachers, and in this respect Jimmy Casas teaches us all that when you work at something you love, it isn't really work at all!"

—**Jana Frieler,** former president of NASSP

"One of the most influential leaders I have ever met comes through with a manifesto that reads as if he were sitting right next to you. From carrying the banner of your school to delivering on the promise a student makes when you believe in them, Jimmy Casas brings passion, purpose, and pride to the world. *Culturize* will not only inspire you to think differently, it will give you the practical tools to empower those around you and build capacity for leadership in your school, district, or community. It's absolutely brilliant and has the opportunity to change the way we look at schools."

—**Joe Sanfelippo,** superintendent, Fall Creek, Wisconsin, author and speaker

"*Culturize Every Student. Every Day. Whatever it Takes* provides leaders and teachers the methods needed to create and cultivate a culture of excellence in their schools. A positive school culture is the result of building caring relationships and modeling the proper growth mindset. Jimmy Casas inspires us to help build an environment that promotes connecting, learning, sharing, and exceeding our expectations. As John E. Lewis stated, 'If not us, then who? If not now, then when?'"

—**Jerry Blumengarten**, @cybraryman1, constant learner

"When I heard that Jimmy Casas was writing a book on school culture, I couldn't wait to get my hands on it. As I started reading it, I couldn't put it down. Within each page I could hear Jimmy's voice guiding, inspiring, and challenging us as teachers and school leaders. I plan to buy copies for my leadership team as soon as it is available and make it our next book study. Thank you for leading the way."

—**Todd Bloomer**, principal, Bradley Middle School, San Antonio, Texas

"Truly exceptional. If there's ever been a book that's lived up to the title 'must-read,' this is the one. Prepare to laugh, learn, and shed a few tears along the way. Culturize feels more like talking with a trusted friend and mentor than reading a book. Jimmy Casas reminds us of the things we're doing well in schools and how to get better in the areas where our students need us most. Best of all, Culturize calls out greatness in a manner that is both visionary and attainable. It is incredibly authentic and surprisingly actionable."

—**Dr. Brad Gustafson**, National Distinguished Principal, author, Renegade Leadership

"Jimmy Casas doesn't just talk the talk, but he has walked the walk. He weaves compelling stories that combine both personal and professional experiences that helped transform his practice. *Culturize* represents a magnificent manifesto where he gives readers a bullseye view of practical strategies to improve the learning culture of any school or district."

—**Eric Sheninger**, senior fellow, International Center for Leadership in Education (ICLE

CUL
TUR
IZE

Every Student. Every Day. Whatever It Takes.

Jimmy Casas

This book is available at special discounts when purchased in quantity for use as premiums, promotions, fundraisers, or for educational use. For inquiries and details, contact the publisher at books@daveburgessconsulting.com.

Published by Dave Burgess Consulting, Inc.
San Diego, CA
http://daveburgessconsulting.com

Cover Design by Genesis Kohler
Editing and Interior Design by My Writers' Connection

Library of Congress Control Number: 2017947007
Paperback ISBN: 978-1-946444-46-2
Ebook ISBN: 978-1-946444-47-9

First Printing: November 2017

CONTENTS

DEDICATION

I dedicate this book to every one of my former students and former co-workers who taught me that the role of a leader is to inspire others to be more than they ever thought they could be.

FOREWORD
by Salome Thomas-EL

When I first learned that Jimmy Casas was writing a book about school culture for teachers and administrators through the eyes of students, staff, and the community, my first thought was, "It's about time!"** For years, school administrators and teachers have expressed the need for improved and engaging culture in our buildings, but do we really want to do the work necessary to create a caring and nurturing staff, build growth mindsets in our students, support collaboration, model trauma-informed leadership, and communicate better with our parents? Those are just a few of the concepts on which we'll need to focus to transform our schools. I am sure we all agree that the work will not be easy, but we know it is necessary. That's why I am gratified that Jimmy decided to write this important book so we would have a valuable resource to help us deal with the rapidly changing leadership challenges we all face. Our lives are so busy and hectic that we often come to depend on roadmaps to help us navigate through the trips, traps, and pitfalls of school leadership and management.

In *Culturize* we are provided a common-sense roadmap to becoming advocates for our students and teachers, creating communities of excellence, taking a stand for positive energy, and living our purpose to maximize our connections with educators around the world. Early in my career as a principal, my primary focus was to be recognized as the popular leader who tried his best to make every teacher happy without considering how it would impact my school's culture and student performance. My school culture and student achievement suffered because I was focused on ensuring that the adults who worked for me were happy and would not complain to the superintendent. What I should have focused on was the well-being of my entire school community. To change those circumstances, I was forced to become a champion for my students and develop better relationships with all the stakeholders in my school.

In this powerful book, you will learn that building a positive school climate and classroom environment is about building effective relationships. The principal and the leadership team must be consistent and committed, no matter the challenges, to fostering positive connections with teachers, students, and parents. Please excuse the basketball reference, but the principal is the point guard in the school—he or she facilitates the culture in the entire school. Principals must make developing strong relationships with teachers a priority, and teachers must develop relationships with their students. When school leaders exhibit a genuine care and concern for students and teachers and expect excellence, it helps to develop long-lasting, meaningful relationships that influence the school culture in a powerful way.

School culture is important. You can walk into any school in the world and know immediately if the students and teachers are engaged, challenged, supported, and happy. All you have to do is feel the energy in the building. If we want to build schools where parents and teachers are fighting to get in instead of out, we must make developing positive school cultures a priority for every school and principal that welcomes children each day. Parents choose schools because of how the adults make children feel. Each and every parent wants a school that is safe, challenging, nurturing, creative, innovative, and fun for their child. Positive school culture and climate helps build resilient children. When students feel they matter and have meaningful participation in school, they become confident that they can overcome the obstacles in their lives.

Creativity, collaboration, and innovation are also important to school culture. School leaders must foster an environment that supports honest communication and creative thinking. Many principal training programs do not focus on the skills and strategies for creating positive school cultures. This training is normally found in management and business schools. The tools Jimmy Casas gives us in this book will launch us to the front of the class and on our way to carrying the banner for our schools and creating more positive school cultures. Principals and teachers can completely transform their schools when they focus on building strong school cultures. Personalized professional development (PD) and team-building opportunities are essential to creating a strong school culture. School districts do their best to provide the necessary PD and training for school staff so they are able to become merchants of hope (this book provides that) and create school cultures that support student and teacher growth. *Culturize* offers guidance for teachers and leaders until they can get much needed support from other sources.

Read and enjoy this book! You will push forward with changing the culture in your school when you are finished. A great culture is like the oxygen in our air—we can't survive without it!

CHAPTER 1
Just Talk to Me

A conversation is so much more than words: a conversation is eyes, smiles, the silences between words.

—Annika Thor

I **still remember the day my baseball coach stopped by my house to pick up my uniform.** I had quit the team out of frustration because I wasn't playing as much as I thought I should be. I had been successful at every level I had played and was the starting center fielder and lead-off hitter for our varsity team until an injury took me out of the line-up. I didn't want to quit, but as a seventeen-year-old kid, I lacked the social and emotional skills and maturity to work through this low point in my life on my own. After all, I was healthy again and felt I deserved to have my starting spot back; instead, I watched game after game from the bench. My parents, who were angry about me not playing more, were not in the best place mentally or emotionally to help me work through my dilemma. Quitting seemed to be the easiest way out, and they didn't try to dissuade me.

The doorbell rang, and I peered through the window to make sure it was him before I opened the door. I remember wishing that my coach would put his arm around me and tell me a story about him knowing how I felt because he, too, had been in a similar situation as a boy. I wanted him to tell me he understood why I was frustrated and then apologize for never talking to me about why I was no longer playing. I wanted him to tell me he wasn't going to let me quit. I wanted him to show me he cared about me—cared enough to tell me to keep my uniform and that he would see me at practice that afternoon. But the words never came; instead, he reached out and grabbed my uniform, shook his head, turned, and walked away. I was devastated. I went straight to my room and cried.

"Why wouldn't he just talk to me?" I kept asking myself.

It's been thirty-two years since that interaction took place on my front door step, but it still serves as an important reminder to me in my work as a school leader to not underestimate how critical it is to take time to talk to students and understand what they see, feel, and experience. I can honestly say that most of what I have learned from working with students has come from—you guessed it—talking with and listening to students. My experience working in schools during the past twenty-five years has taught me that most of the conversations had by adults in schools today are barely scratching the surface or, worse, come packaged with a tone that reflects an adult-centered culture. In many cases we adults sometimes avoid interacting with students altogether, either because we are too busy, we are not sure what to say, or we're afraid of saying the wrong thing, just like my baseball coach did. This leaves students walking school hallways every day feeling invisible and wishing someone would just take the time to talk to them in a genuine and caring way.

Consider this scenario as but one example:

As Ebony walked into the school building, she had a sinking feeling in her stomach. It was November, and she had just moved into a new community. She was nervous about starting a new school midway through the school year. This was her first day of school; she kept her eyes down, nervous, not knowing what to expect as she walked into the main office. Suddenly, the office secretary called out to her in a tone that made her skip a breath. "Where are you supposed to be? Do you have a pass? Move on now before the tardy bell rings and the vice principal gives you a detention for being late."

This scenario is playing out each day in schools across the country. It may come across as somewhat exaggerated, but if you have spent any amount of time in a school environment, you have probably witnessed such an interaction. And this is the kind of interaction that has led to me to ponder these questions:

- Have we reached the point where we are willing to allow an average, typical culture to determine our students' or schools' potential for success?

- What if we were to pause, step back, and view our culture through the eyes of every child, every day?

- Are we willing to do whatever it takes to *culturize* our schools to a level that defines excellence?

The thought of schools using measures of success based on the status quo is frightening, especially when we consider what a mediocre culture means for our children, our teachers, our schools, and ultimately for our school communities. As I began this work on examining the critical role educators play in "culturizing" schools, I asked teachers, support staff, principals, and superintendents alike the following question: **"Where does average exist in your organization?"**

What I admired most about the educators who responded to my question was that they were willing to admit that yes, average exists in offices, classrooms, hallways, cafeterias, practice fields, and schools in general. Most of the time they pointed to themselves first when identifying the areas where average lives within their own practices. They also recognized that their approach (average or otherwise) impacts the very fiber of the school culture in which they serve. If we were all to be completely honest and willing to own our shortcomings, we could all say that we have, at one time or another, played a role in fostering a culture that was average at best—or worse, less than average.

As school teachers and leaders, it is our responsibility to prohibit average from becoming our standard. We must take time to reflect on and be willing to be vigilant in examining our school cultures through the eyes of students and staff and ask, "What role are we playing in *culturizing* our schools?" Taking responsibility for cultural dilemmas is a good start, but it's only the first step. Once we've identified the source of the problem, the question we should ask is this: What are we doing about it? Until we take action, nothing changes.

CULTURIZE: To cultivate a community of learners by behaving in a kind, caring, honest, and compassionate manner in order to challenge and inspire each member of the school community to become more than they ever thought possible.

The Biggest Challenge Facing Schools Today

In early 2017 I was conducting a workshop on the topic of school leadership, and I posed the following question to school administrators who were attending: **What do you believe to be the biggest issue facing us today in public education that is resulting in many of our schools being labeled as low performing?**

The question elicited several interesting responses. Here are a few of the most common reasons that were presented:

- Standardized Testing
- State and Federal Mandates
- Lack of Funding, Resources
- Teacher Evaluation System/Accountability
- Micro-Managing School Boards
- Teacher Turnover/Shortage
- Poverty
- Poor Parenting
- Mental Health Issues

I wasn't surprised by the responses. Quite frankly, the answers I get generally follow a similar pattern. Standardized testing and state and federal mandates usually lead the way with funding shortages following closely behind. I must admit I always hesitate when I get to this segment of my presentation for fear of offending someone, but then again, I believe I owe it to the audience to try to keep the conversation real. To affect change, we must be honest—with one another and ourselves; we must be willing to reflect on our own leadership.

The question is simply a starting place for the tough conversations and honest reflection that need to happen. You see, I don't believe any items from the list above are our biggest pitfalls. It is easy to point to external factors that might be causing our organizations—or more specifically student and teacher performance—to fall short of expectations. One of the hardest places to look when things aren't going as well as we hoped is at ourselves and our own attitudes, practices, and skill sets, especially if it means examining the influence we have. When it comes to measuring the culture of our schools and success of our students and staff, there really is only one place to look when we fall short: our own ability to lead effectively.

Everyone Is a Leader

I believe that ineffective leadership is the biggest issue facing not only public education but small businesses and large companies alike. Look around and you will see dozens of schools being labeled as poor performing along with businesses, including restaurants, retail stores, and banks, closing as a result of poor leadership. My intent is not to place the blame solely on the shoulders of school and district leaders. I recall speaking to a group of district teachers during a workshop when I shared with them that I believed the biggest issue facing us today in public schools was ineffective leadership. The rousing cheers and applause from the teachers in the audience completely caught me off guard. Clearly, to them, "leadership" meant "building administration." I gathered my thoughts, looked out into the audience, and quietly stated, "I wasn't talking about the administration. I was talking about all of you—collectively—teacher and school leaders alike. You see, everyone here has the capacity to lead, and everyone here is responsible for the culture and climate of your organization. No one person is responsible for determining your success or failure but you, and no one is responsible for your morale but you." On the flight home, I couldn't help but reflect on the response of the audience. I hoped my message of collective impact and personal responsibility had resonated with them.

> **No one person is responsible for determining your success or failure but you, and no one is responsible for your morale but you.**

When I was a principal, I wanted our teachers and support staff to feel valued and appreciated. I held myself accountable for the successes and failures of my students and staff, always reflecting on what I could have done differently or more effectively to help them feel as though they were experiencing the success they desired. Their failures were my failures.

Great Leaders Inspire Greatness

One day as I was perusing my social media feed, I became involved in an exchange in which I stated that no one went into teaching to be average, and those who were had simply lost their way. I then followed this statement with the comment that great leaders can inspire average teachers back to greatness. That follow-up piece drew the attention of an acquaintance who stated I could not have been more wrong. My acquaintance and I had obviously had different experiences, which led to a healthy discussion about the power of leadership and the struggles leaders face. My belief that leaders have the power to influence others and draw out the best in them is rooted in personal experience and in the examples I've seen and heard about from others. Through the years I have watched talented individuals excel at high levels. I have listened and learned from genuine people who inspired me and motivated me to become more than I ever thought possible. Yes, it was ultimately up to me to take these words and initiate my own action, but I also know that my desire to move forward in an attempt to push myself toward excellence was ignited by these individuals' words or actions. As someone who prides himself on being able to support others in their quest for personal excellence, it is my *choice* to believe that leaders can inspire greatness in others. That belief alone does not define a leader's effectiveness, but given the choice, wouldn't you prefer to work for a leader who aspires to make such an impact? I would! After all, don't we expect our teachers to believe that change, growth, and excellence are possible for their students? And if we expect unwavering belief and determination from our staff toward our students, shouldn't we model the behaviors and attitudes we want to see?

The plethora of issues facing education today can burden us and in some cases even paralyze us or tempt us to blame others for our lack of success. I recognize that being an effective leader is not simply about being able to inspire others through words or actions. Nothing is that simple, especially when it comes to leadership. But I became a teacher and a school leader because I wanted to inspire others to join me in the quest to develop the qualities and characteristics of great leaders. My guess is that you had similar reasons for moving into the classroom or school administration. And if our goal is to help others become great leaders—in our classrooms, offices, buildings, districts, and communities—as we seek to continually improve personally, then I think we are on the right path to identifying, addressing, and remedying any shortfalls we have as leaders.

More than ever, I am convinced that leadership matters. It matters a lot. Everyone has the capacity to lead, and we need our best people leading. The longer we stay in the trenches as leaders, the more we understand that the difference between today and tomorrow is *us*. It's as simple as that. For those of us who are in leadership roles in schools, it is our responsibility to identify where average exists, and it is our obligation to actually change it, not just manage it. The same is true of teachers who lead their classrooms, athletic coaches who work with student athletes, superintendents who lead our schools, and of course, school boards who oversee our districts.

Too often, however, we get stuck in the habit of simply managing a mediocre culture. Challenging the status quo can seem daunting and overwhelming. I get that; I really do. If we aren't careful, fighting something so entrenched can drain us of our energy, create undue stress, impact our mood, and even negatively affect our mindset. Because of the demands placed on our profession, it can be easy to lose our sense of passion, our sense of purpose, and our sense of pride. If (or when) this happens, we run the risk of going from mere management of the school culture to becoming a negative impact. We must remain vigilant that our words and deeds add to our school culture in a positive way rather than negate it. Consider the following questions as you think about the influence you have on your school or classroom:

- Do your words inspire others for success or shame?

- Do your actions result in wellness or weariness?

- Do you dismiss the needs of others?

- Do you dismiss the gifts of others?

Wherever you are in terms of how you are impacting your school's culture—for good or ill—in the chapters that follow, you'll be inspired to become a champion for those with whom you work, teach, and lead.

Go Beyond Technical Excellence

The challenges and expectations for educators are daunting. Developing and implementing a rigorous and relevant curriculum, differentiating instruction to meet diverse individual student needs, and communicating effectively with parents are just the tip of the expectations. Add a deep understanding of personal student situations, ability to secure community-based services for students and families, and compassion for individual circumstances, and it's obvious the demands placed on educators are immense. Sure, educators would like to (and should) be paid more. After all, I don't know too many other professions where employees are asked to do twelve months' worth of work in nine months and then turn around and prep for the next three months to be ready to do it all again. We would like to be more respected, revered, and valued. But to be an excellent educator is a gift—a gift to our students, our families, and our communities. Being an excellent educator is, in fact, a gift to our humanity.

> **To be an excellent educator is a gift—a gift to our students, our families, and our communities. Being an excellent educator is, in fact, a gift to our humanity.**

Designing curriculum, instruction, and assessment is critical to preparing students for success, but equally imperative to student achievement is the culture and atmosphere in which students learn. My goal with this book is to challenge the thinking regarding school culture and to inspire educators everywhere—including you—to consider ways to improve it; for example...

- Does your school have unified expectations throughout your culture regarding how the adults treat the students and their families?

- Is there a positive and caring cultural standard regarding the relationships between the adults and the students and among the adults themselves?

- Do the practices and policies of your organization point to a student-centered culture rooted in kindness and compassion?

- Do the adults in your school treat students in a manner that positively contributes to your school becoming a community?

- Do the beliefs, attitudes, behaviors, and interactions of your staff with students and with each other scream, "I care about you!", "You can do better!", and "You are important to me!"?

Eyes on Culture by Nicholas Ferroni

Social Studies Teacher, Union High School, Union, New Jersey

As educators, we know that so many students come to school for so much more than just an education. Students who are loved at home come to school to learn, and those who aren't, come to school to be loved. I have found that the most effective teachers are not the ones who know the most but the ones who care the most.

One great example is a former student, Kandon, whom I met during his sophomore year while I was helping out with the football team. To be honest, Kandon was very angry and aggressive. For some reason he just didn't seem like a happy child and was always quick to be confrontational with both classmates and teachers. Though I never had Kandon as an actual student, during the school year I would always talk to him, and we even started staying after practice to work on football drills. Little by little, Kandon began to let down his guard and open up. He shared how his mother passed away when he was very little and his father never really cared about him, and it was his grandmother who filled the nurturing role. Slowly, Kandon, this six-foot-three-inch, two-hundred-thirty-pound football player, began to smile, laugh, and show signs of compassion that were not apparent when I first met him. I even started training Kandon and a group of students at the gym daily, where we had some great moments and developed a powerful bond. Kandon became like my little brother and slowly became the amazing young man that was there the whole time. By his senior year, his grades had improved and he even was able to get into Rutgers, which was the school he had always wanted to attend. Watching him grow and become the amazing young man he is today is truly one of my proudest moments as an educator.

Over the years, we met up, trained, and always stayed in touch—I helped him with college tuition on a few occasions and encouraged him to stay on the path. Though I knew we had a great relationship, it didn't really hit me until Kandon graduated from Rutgers with honors and we went out to celebrate. Kandon told me that if it wasn't for me taking time to talk to him and mentor him— never giving up on him when he had his bad days—he would not have graduated, and he wouldn't have gone to college. He then added that he might not even be alive today. Of course, I get a little emotional when I tell his story. I'm not saying this to brag that I am such an amazing teacher or should be sainted. (To be honest, Kandon is a survivor and a fighter, and I know he would have made it through.) I'm sharing this because I didn't do anything exceptional; I just cared about a student when he needed it most.

In my fifteen years as an educator, I can proudly say that I have encountered many similar stories of students who thanked their teachers for caring when they didn't even care about themselves, for believing in them when they seemed hopeless. Teachers can't replace parents, but so many students are saved by teachers who assume the role when there is a vacancy. I honestly believe that the three most important characteristics of an amazing educator are compassion, passion, and knowledge. In that exact order.

The Four Core Principles of Positive School Culture

An excellent culture is critical to the success of any organization. Throughout this book, I will share experiences and thoughts regarding organizational values and how to culturize your school by following a framework built on a fundamental set of four core principles, sometimes intentionally and well, sometimes unintentionally. I believe organizational core values are the foundation of all school cultures and therefore are critical to the success of any organization, especially those that refuse to let status quo become their standard. I will expand on these four core principles in the subsequent chapters of this book. For now, here is a brief summary of the four core principles that distinguish a culturalized school through the eyes of the entire school community.

To start, we must expect all staff to **champion for all students.** I think we must always begin with the belief that kids *can*. Period. Teachers and leaders who have transformed their belief systems to acquire such a mindset are never deterred by failure or the unknown. They stay the course and focus on the long term rather than the short term, recognizing that it is their moral imperative to advocate for all students until they are ready to experience personal success. These forward-thinking educators remain motivated by hope and faith. They are more than motivated; they act on that hope and faith in ways that inspire others to do the same.

Next, every staff member must **expect excellence** of one another and, most importantly, of their students. It is my belief that all kids, regardless of race, socio-economic class, ethnicity, sexual orientation, perceived ability, attitude, etc., should be held to the highest standard for learning when it comes to their academics and/or their behavior. By not holding all students to a high standard, we are saying we don't believe you are able to learn or act appropriately, or we don't care whether you do. *Why would we accept anything but our students' best?* It is usually the result of a student's perceived attitude or poor behavior that school personnel use as an excuse to give up on a child. In my experience, the children who are most susceptible to having adults give up on them are poor or minority students, or they are students who struggle with self-discipline, or they have lost confidence. These students' body language often communicates they have quit. We can't quit on them. We must not give up on those students who need us most.

In addition to being a champion for all students and expecting excellence, all staff members must **carry the banner** for their school in a positive light at all times. We are all—students, staff, and parents—responsible for contributing a positive voice. By not carrying the banner for our schools in a positive light, we begin to lose our sense of pride, our identity, and our desire to invest in our community. We must support one another by making sure we are taking time to lift each other up and to understand that it is never about us; it is about serving others and serving the greater good.

Finally, every educator, administrator, and support staff member must strive to **be a merchant of hope.** We may not get to decide which kids to serve, but we do get to decide the kind of climate in

> **We may not get to decide which kids to serve, but we do get to decide the kind of climate in which we want to serve them.**

which we want to serve them. **Every child deserves the opportunity to be a part of something great**, and we must find ways to make an impact both individually and collectively. What we do as educators will leave a lasting impression on the lives of our students, staff, and school communities. That is the beauty and the responsibility of what we do. We serve in a profession where we are blessed every day with the opportunity to help change the course of someone's life with our words, our actions, and our belief in their abilities. By changing our perspectives, we can change lives.

> **We are blessed every day with the opportunity to help change the course of someone's life with our words, our actions, and our belief in their abilities. By changing our perspectives, we can change lives.**

Simply put, we cannot allow average to become our standard. Our kids deserve more than the status quo; they deserve our very best! The primary purpose of this book is to assist all educators, administrators, and support staff members in exploring their mindset, skills, attributes, and behaviors as well as the role we each play in creating a less-than-average, average, or excellent school culture. It's also framed to get you to reflect on your practices and to help you recognize where your personal average exists so as to inspire you and move you to take action with a sense of urgency. Our goal should be to create schools and communities that equip young people in developing skills, habits, and competencies that produce an educated citizenry rooted in healthy, personalized, and productive relationships.

This book is not a step-by-step or how-to guide. As I share my experiences as a learner and leader, I hope to illustrate how a vibrant culture can produce uplifting energy, create positive change, and produce a genuine and caring experience for every member of a school community. We must remember that the amount of time students and staff spend in school is just a small fraction of their lives, but it is a part that will stick with them forever, just like that moment with my coach on my front porch has stuck with me for so many years. In each chapter, you will find "Eyes on Culture" excerpts from current educators in the field who aspire to model by example the four core principles that distinguish a culturized school of excellence. At the end of each chapter, you will find proven **culture builders** to support you in your quest to culturize your classroom, school, and/or community. My hope is that this book will inspire you to do your part to ensure a successful, rewarding, caring, and positive school experience for every student, every day, and more importantly, that you are willing to do whatever it takes to make it happen.

We cannot allow average to become our standard.

QUESTIONS FOR DISCUSSION

» Where does average currently exist in your school or district?

» What are you doing about it? What average can you address first?

» When did you last try something for the very first time? How did it make you feel? Are there students and staff who harbor the same feelings? If so, why? What does this tell us about our culture?

» What would you do differently if you were not afraid? What is keeping you from going for it?

CHAPTER 2
CORE PRINCIPLE 1:
Champion for Students

The moment you're ready to quit is usually the moment right before a miracle happens. Don't give up.

—Unknown

You probably know a few educators who embody this first core principle of championing for kids. You see them daily encouraging the silent girls, believing in the mischievous boys, building up those who lack confidence, seeking out the entitled, the poor, the incarcerated, the gifted, the reluctant learners, and those struggling with their sexuality. They are intentional about doing whatever it takes to help each of them become their personal best. Perhaps you are one of these passionate teachers or administrators who relentlessly holds on to and intentionally lives out of a deep belief that connecting with kids and valuing their talents and voices is the first step to creating the kind of school culture and experiences that will impact students for a lifetime. I certainly hope so. But even if you feel like you aren't quite there yet, the fact that you're reading this book indicates to me that you care deeply about your students. And that's where becoming a champion begins.

It Begins with Us

When I was five years old, my father would take me and my then ten-year-old brother to work with him on the weekends. He served as a custodian for the school district, and each Saturday morning we joined my father as he made his rounds through the schools. I often joke that my father broke every child labor law in existence, often requiring us to help clean for hours on end. My jobs consisted of emptying trash cans, erasing chalkboards, cleaning restrooms, and sweeping and mopping classrooms, hallways, and locker rooms. My favorite job was sweeping the gymnasium floor with a push broom that was bigger than me. Although my dad demanded a lot from us and expected us to perform our "duties" at a high level, he was always right there cleaning alongside us and modeling exactly how he wanted each task done. And if we didn't do it the way he expected, he wouldn't do it for us; instead, he would show us (again) how to do the job and then help us rather than make us do it alone.

Later, my parents got into the movie theater and restaurant businesses, and work became the norm for us Casas boys. These were family businesses, which meant we served in every possible role: ticket sellers, ticket takers, concession-stand workers, gophers, custodians, hosts, waiters, cooks, inventory recorders, maintenance helpers, accountants, and yes, once again, custodians. During these critical seventeen years of my life (from age five to twenty-two), my parents instilled in me a sense of pride, the value of a strong work ethic and community, and an understanding that if I wanted something in this world, it was my responsibility to make it happen. They taught my brothers and me that if we made hard work our passion, then we would be successful regardless of what career we chose. And even though my parents did everything they could to help us understand this way of life, regrettably, their efforts fell short on me, their middle child. I worked hard in our family businesses, but these values did not transfer to my schoolwork.

If you've heard me speak or have read my blog, you probably already know that I did not have a positive school experience. My high school counselors never encouraged me to take an honors course or fill out a college application. I didn't understand the significance of the ACT, and I thought an AP course was a class taught by the assistant principal. I don't recall my counselors in junior high asking me about my interests outside of school, what my passions were, or even what skills I thought I possessed. By the end of my seventh-grade year, most of my teachers had labeled me a "troublemaker." I spent most of my days in in-school suspension, Room 202, isolated from my classmates. I then carried my poor attitude and apathy into high school. My struggles continued, and I became so disengaged with school that it was commonplace for me to disrupt the lesson and, as a result, get kicked out of class and straight into detention. My parents had hopes and dreams of me making the honor roll, but my GPA was abysmal.

In high school I met an assistant principal by the name of Mr. Morgan. He was a kind gentleman who always made time for me and treated me in a respectful and caring way, even though I often behaved in a manner that didn't lend itself to sympathetic treatment. I grew to respect and admire Mr. Morgan, and it was that relationship that proved to be my saving grace when I was expelled from high school my senior year for getting into a fight with my PE teacher. In my mind, the fight was justified. He had called me a "dirty Mexican" and slammed me to the ground for refusing to obey his orders. Getting expelled was one more wound to my already discouraged and disillusioned psyche. Mr. Morgan was one of the few people who advocated for me at the time. He helped my parents navigate an appeals process that was completely foreign to them. Eventually, I was reinstated by the board, and with the support of a few caring teachers, I graduated that year.

My poor attitude and disengagement with school continued into my college years, leading first to academic probation and then eventually to my quitting school altogether. The irony of it all was that, throughout my school experience, I was labeled as a lazy, angry kid who had a chip on his shoulder. Looking back, I can see why I was labeled as such, but the diagnosis could not have been further from the truth. Lazy? Not a chance. In fact, I loved to work; I just didn't love to work in school unless it was beside my father as his custodial helper. And a chip on my shoulder? Maybe, but I just wanted my teachers to understand why I wasn't doing the work. I wanted them to hold me to a high standard, not turn away and tell another adult I wasn't worth it. I wanted them to see that I lacked the confidence and belief that I could do the work. I wanted them to know I wasn't lazy or undisciplined. Fortunately for me, Mr. Morgan had taken the time to get to know me enough that he was able to see through my lack of confidence and recognize that somewhere inside was a kid with talent and skills who just needed the right structure and support to go on to do great things. That's why he was willing to be an advocate—a champion—for me. He saw in me more than I could see in myself.

Unfulfilled Expectations

I will admit it: Even though I know how I respond is my choice, there have been—and still are—moments in which I didn't choose the best response. No one is immune. After all, we are not superhuman. We are people with feelings, and sometimes we take things personally and let them affect us in ways that cause us to get down on ourselves and respond in inappropriate ways at inopportune times. One of my repeat triggers for a less-than-ideal response was working with adults who made decisions or behaved in ways that indicated they cared more about themselves than what was in the best interest of our students. During my tenure as both a teacher and as a principal, there were days where my frustration grew because I wanted to save every student, and I knew I couldn't do it alone. Each year I extended my streak of "losing" kids, and those losses killed me. Adding a student's name to the failure or dropout list never got easier. For someone who took great pride in being a champion for kids, it was a hard pill to swallow.

In those difficult professional moments when I was struggling and questioning my impact as an educator, I often turned to writing and blogging to talk myself out of giving up. Not only did the act of thinking through my frustrations and writing about it help me reframe what was possible, but I like to think it was also a way for me to support my colleagues throughout my state and across the country whom I knew experienced that same sick feeling when a student was ready to give up and walk away. There were days, weeks, months, and even years when I gave all my emotional energy to my students (and in most cases, their families). When they hurt, I hurt. After more than two decades as a school administrator, I still couldn't avoid it. I wanted to see every student reach their full potential. I didn't want them living in a prison of poor choices. I wanted to see our students reach their potential freedom so they could experience firsthand the joy and feeling that comes with accomplishing something significant.

Some days tested my resilience as a school leader as I struggled to help students deal with their ongoing personal crises. I recall one conversation where a student shared he didn't believe I cared about him. Another student spoke of being on a path of self-destruction and feeling like there wasn't anyone who could help him. A sophomore boy felt like the school system was placing limits on his academic abilities. Another young lady described how she walked the hallways after each class period with hundreds of students yet felt as though the hallways were empty and she was alone. And finally, for one young man, school was still a place where a team of adults came together like a parole board to determine his future.

The feelings of turmoil for my students often caused me to reflect on my personal student experience. I felt like I understood their struggles, because I, too, had struggled in school. In fact, my personal experiences served as my motivation for becoming a school leader; I wanted to use them to help others. I know that every student has the potential to make a positive impact, so when I felt like I was not able to make a difference with a student, it was hard not to take it personally. I don't mean that I thought their struggles had anything to do with me, but that I personally felt helpless when I was unable to come up with a solution to help a student who was feeling hopeless and lost.

I know from conversations with some students, they still believed school was an "institution" which put limits on their potential. They shared stories of being told for years they couldn't do this or they couldn't do that. They believed the system categorized them throughout their school experience and labeled them as average, low-ability reader, at-risk, potential dropout, special needs, etc. At the same time, they watched the same "institution" label others as honor students, talented and gifted, college bound, and as possessing AP potential. Some students have shared stories of unfulfilled promises by adults and a system which assured them of success only to find out they meant success for those who were willing to play the game of school and who were compliant. Some of these students attended school in body but were absent in mind and in spirit. In other words, they had checked out and were just hanging around the prison yard of lost potential waiting to escape.

Eyes on Culture by Robert Sigrist

Principal, Savannah High School, Savannah, Missouri

It is a moral and ethical imperative that we be champions for all students. As leaders, we must model this for others, never wavering in that core belief. We must persevere when we might be deterred by a lack of short-term results, keeping the long-term success of students in mind, even as they reject our efforts. When you are truly committed to being a champion for all students, you stay motivated to helping them achieve that goal, whether it be acceptance at a prestigious university, graduating from high school, or staying in school when they want to drop out, knowing that each of those successes are equally important to the individual. I've seen students succeed in each of these situations, and I'm reminded of a former student who had little motivation, didn't care about school, and was making poor choices away from school, even ones that threatened her health and safety. Being a champion for her meant continuing to encourage her, to remain firm in that belief, even when she declined all help and was lost in drugs at one point. Additionally, it was not something accomplished by one person. I teamed with her mother and counselor, all of us together trying to provide support. Teachers were encouraged to keep working with her as she finally started to take some interest in school work. Being a champion for her was not something done alone; it involved motivating others to champion for her. By continuing to reach out to her, to push her, and to help her see her potential, she eventually found her way. Today she is a college graduate and a social worker, paying it forward by being a champion for others. As a champion for all students, their success becomes how you base your own. Being a champion for all students means just that: all students. Not just ones who are likeable and want help but also the ones who might resist your efforts. Even then, your core values drive you to stay true to this belief. This unwavering hope and faith can be the model to inspire others to do the same for all students.

You have probably seen students walking the halls at your school who, though physically there, by every other measure of existence have checked out. They are the students labeled as apathetic, disenfranchised, lazy, struggling, or even as "reluctant learners." So what happened to them? Where did their interest in school and learning go? Why did it disappear? When did it happen? In most cases, the answer to that last question is not high school. The difficulty many students experience in school began as early as elementary school. These are students who read below grade level, who don't "get" math, who experience high levels of anxiety taking tests, who don't fit into any peer group, or the ones whose struggles often lead to the initial stages of a free fall that continues into middle school and high school until they hit rock bottom. Hence, it is imperative that we begin early on to implement in our schools systemic, organized structures to ensure that every child feels safe, connected, and valued by staff and that our programs accommodate a diverse group of learners. We must put practices into place that invite and support family engagement and provide resources for strong early childhood literacy. We must implement programs for mentoring and tutoring our students as they advance in grade level along with after-school programs to support extended learning opportunities for all students. I understand that the issues teachers and administrators are facing can seem insurmountable, but we must stay the course and continue to improve school for our students.

As I stated in the introduction, I believe that all children need a champion who cares about them and is willing to encourage them. But they also need someone to take notice of their skills and then provide them with the strategies and an understanding of how to use those skill sets to thrive. In our most challenged students' lives, myriad variables factor into why some succeed and others don't. Many come to school regularly feeling all alone, compounded by negative expectations about themselves and their circumstances. In some instances they're harboring negative feelings about the institution of school itself. As educators, we have the power to change these expectations by building meaningful relationships with all students. We can achieve this by focusing on the "three Rs": relationships...relationships...relationships. Getting to know our students on a more personal level, such as their interests, fears, and talents is vital to creating a classroom culture where every child feels valued and understood; however, too often we stay near the surface treading water rather than diving deeper. By doing so, we stop short of the next crucial step of any relationship, and that is allowing the students to get to know us. I don't mean get to know us only in terms of our personal lives. I mean that we invite them in to see our core. What drives us to do what we do? What gets us up in the morning and pushes us to want to teach? From what do we draw to make our decisions? It is imperative that our students know our core principles so they know what to expect. More importantly, they need to understand what we value so they can see our behaviors mirror our beliefs. Finally, the last and final piece of the relationship pyramid is creating an environment where the students get to know one another. Only by intentionally taking time to invest in activities that allow students to regularly interact with one another can we ever achieve the classroom culture of excellence we all aspire to attain: An atmosphere where all students understand, appreciate, respect, and empathize with one another. When we champion for students in this manner, they begin to not only expect more from us, they learn to expect more from themselves.

Relationships

Relationships

Relationships

I believe we must invest in the three Rs on a daily basis so all kids feel like they belong. Our students deserve our very best, and we need to continue to fight for every one of them, even if we know full well that we can't save them all. A dear friend and principal mentor of mine, Dr. Donder, who gave me my first assistant principal job, often said to me, "Jimmy, everyone has a savior, but it isn't always going to be you." Then after a brief pause he would say, "But it doesn't give you an excuse not to try." He taught me early on that it was not my place to judge a student's contribution to our school community, but it was my job to provide a means for them to share their skills and talents. It was also my job to help them acquire the necessary skills and strategies to improve their chances of not walking out as a prisoner of potential but rather as the embodiment of promised expectations fulfilled.

Inhibited by the 3 Cs

I do believe it's true that every child has unlimited potential, but I know from my own school experience as well as through my experiences as a teacher and a principal that many students don't recognize their own potential. I have spent a great deal of time working with students whom others label as "reluctant learners." I know some educators would categorize these students as apathetic due to an apparent absence of interest or lack of concern about school. Sadly, some educators would go so far as to say these students are incapable of doing "grade-level" work. I'm not minimizing the reality that some students aren't living up to their potential, nor do I debate the fact that the students who struggle with learning sometimes prove to be the most challenging in our classrooms. But I do wonder if it has to be that way.

I can recall countless times in school when I felt as if I didn't belong, or that I wasn't smart enough, or that maybe school just wasn't for me. When I take time to reflect on my entire school experience, I can recognize that I did not always feel that way. In fact, I cherished my elementary school experience. My best school memories revolved around my elementary school days and can be attributed to my teachers who truly believed in and cared about me. They left such an impression on me that I returned to my hometown a few years back to attend a retirement luncheon for three of my elementary school teachers. So what happened? It is hard for me to pinpoint the exact time or year that things began to unwind for me personally. What I can tell you is that my high school and undergraduate college experiences left in me a confidence void which still impacts me as a learner today.

One of my goals as an educator has been to talk with kids, to get to understand them, and in doing so, try to make sense of why some kids are more successful than others. Through those conversations

I've identified three interrelated areas that either propel or inhibit a child's success in school:

- **Connection.** Many students have shared with me they do not feel connected at school. They want to have meaningful and purposeful relationships with their teachers and their principals but instead feel complete disconnection.

    When educators sustain a connection with children throughout their entire school experience, the positive impact is profound. As champions for students, our responsibility is to put systems into place to ensure that all—not just some—students are cared for on a more personal level at school. The word "systems" may seem cold, but the reality is that unless we are intentional about creating connection with children, someone will fall through the cracks.

- **Capability.** Students very often take their cues regarding their beliefs about their own capability from their teachers. When students overhear a teacher say, "I don't think she can do this," or "He isn't AP material," they believe it and settle at a level of average (or below) rather than pushing to reach excellence.

    We either believe that all students have the potential to learn at a level that reflects success, or we don't. My observation of schools tells me we still have some teachers, administrators, parents, and students who don't believe success is possible, not for some, but for *all* kids. When an educator shakes his head and says, "I don't think they can learn this," I feel a stab of pain and a jolt of defensiveness because I remember my own school days when I struggled and wanted so badly to be able to show my teachers and professors I *could* do it; I just needed their help. I needed them to sit next to me and watch me as I struggled to read or complete my work so they could offer me guidance. At the same time, I wanted them to share my excitement when I accomplished a task or completed a problem so they could see I was capable of doing the work with their support.

- **Confidence.** Lack of confidence, in my opinion, is the number one reason kids fail. Whether it's in the area of academics, fine arts, or athletics, the inability to believe in oneself is a major contributing factor to failure (whether that means failing a class, a grade level, or dropping out of school completely).

  The key to success for students is to build up their confidence to the level they believe they can learn or achieve anything they put their minds to. A growth mindset, complimented with a strong work ethic and determination, helps ensure students' success in school and in life. It's our job to help students to develop those traits. One way we can do this is by raising the bar for students when they feel stuck or are on the verge of giving up. Our students don't need us feeling sorry for them. Empathy, yes. Sympathy, no. Keep pushing them, but continue to offer support and encouragement while doing so. Put yourself in their shoes. Then pull back and reteach the concept that had been challenging and see how they begin to see that they can do it. We know that good teaching spirals, often introducing new material and challenges. Good teaching also revisits material that was previously covered to build students' confidence and show them they can do it. Students can accomplish any task with the right support and the right attitude.

> *"You only need one person to
> believe in you to succeed. It's a
> lot easier if that person is you."*
>
> —ANONYMOUS

Regardless of students' personal history or circumstances (good or bad), we can help them overcome obstacles by creating a school culture that makes them feel connected, capable, and confident in their abilities. If we want kids to take responsibility for their own learning, we must provide an environment where their curiosity is nurtured and developed—where they want to learn simply for the sake of learning. Unleashing true potential begins by removing the labels that hold children hostage. If we, as teachers and leaders, choose not to act and banish the idea that students are apathetic or uninterested in learning, then we are the reluctant ones.

> **Unleashing true potential begins by removing the labels that hold children hostage.**

Fair Means Treating Students Differently

Have you ever heard a teacher make the following comment? "Well, it is not fair to the other students if I start making exceptions for this student who didn't even try to do the work." Or another example, "It is not fair to the other kids who turned in their work on time if I allow this student to receive credit even though they didn't care enough to do it the first time around." What is interesting about these comments is the word "fair." Rick Wormeli, in his book, *Fair Isn't Always Equal*, addresses this very topic to help us better understand the importance of leveling the playing field for all kids, especially for our struggling learners. It doesn't need to be all or nothing. In discussing late work, Wormeli makes the point that, regarding students who have already proven themselves as proficient or at mastery level, we hold them accountable to a certain level of meeting deadlines because they learned the material, the skill or content. But there is a different frame of reference when you are first teaching students something they need to learn to become proficient. Are we going to hold someone who is not proficient, who is struggling, to the same level of accountability as that of someone who has already mastered the content? Wormeli believes we shouldn't.

A few years ago, I found myself in a situation in which I felt strongly that I needed to advocate for a student with an Individualized Education Plan (IEP). His parent was told, with two-and-a-half weeks left in the marking period, that her child was likely to fail the course. My intent is not to be critical about what the teacher did or didn't do, but rather to reveal what I learned from that experience and what I wish we had done differently as a team of educators:

1. **Seek to understand why the student won't do the work.**
   I have had hundreds of "reluctant learners" tell me they didn't care if they passed or not. I hear their words—and the fear and bravado behind them. The reality is that no child *wants* to be a failure. What these challenged students are really saying is that they lack the skills and/or the confidence to be successful. Admittedly, other factors may come into play, such as a lack of self-discipline, work ethic, or a

commitment to overcome challenges. I would argue, however, that these factors are related to the students' lack of belief in their abilities to do the work (and perhaps recognizing they lack the basic skills) which then results in what appears to be an apathetic attitude toward the subject matter or school in general.

Establishing a trusting relationship with struggling students first allows them to feel comfortable enough to share their personal struggles. This kind of relationship is a must if you are going to help students experience success. So how can we build that kind of trust? It develops with every interaction we have with our students. If you are wondering if your students trust you, here are a few questions to evaluate the way you interact with students—and thereby their level of trust with you:

- Are you honest with your students?

- Are you dependable in following through when you promise to do something?

- Are you available when you say you will be?

- Do you demonstrate a sense of empathy when students hesitate to do what you ask or fail to follow through on what you agreed upon?

- Do you take time to ask questions when they let you down rather than make assumptions regarding the reasons why?

- Are you impeccable with your word?

All these are major factors in earning the trust of our students (and colleagues) so we can better support them on their trek toward success.

2. **Maintain ongoing communication with the parents whose children are struggling.** There is no excuse for not contacting a parent whose student is failing a class. In fact, there should be ongoing communication that focuses on working together to help the student be successful. Even when we recognize early on that the parent(s) is/are not able to help, we as a staff should maintain communication as a courtesy. I often communicated to teachers that, since the difficult conversation was inevitable, it was better to have it earlier rather than after the student had failed (which gives the conversation a completely different tone). And let me add that the most effective communication is face-to-face or by phone. Email or text conversations can go south in a hurry, so I urge educators to avoid those modes of communication when discussing a student's poor performance with parents.

3. **Recognize that it is okay to ask for help. Sometimes talking to the student isn't enough.** The amount of support that some students need for even the smallest of gains in learning can feel overwhelming. This is reason enough to accept the fact that the toll on one person may be too great. We must be willing to look at a student who is failing despite all our best efforts and recognize that something needs to change. In the scenario I described above, at least six adults played a part in watching a student fail, yet they all believed they had done all they could to help the student be successful. When asked specifically what they had done to help the student be successful, all responded by saying they had talked to the student and told him what he needed to do to pass the class. What we as a teaching team failed to do was get all six adults together in a room with the parent and

> the student and come to an agreement about 1) what success would look like for this student and 2) identify what support the student would need in order to be successful, including what role the student would need to play in his own success.

The situation literally made me sick to my stomach. My heart went out to this student because I recognized that, as a system, we had failed him. I also knew that my staff had the best of intentions and felt they were pushing him along and encouraging him to do what he needed to do to pass the class. The student, however, had not taken responsibility for his own learning and he would now have to learn a tough lesson. I knew the right thing to do was to have a conversation with each person and explain where, in my opinion, we had failed the student. Those weren't conversations I looked forward to. I knew I would take some hits along the way because some teachers would not feel supported. Some would feel it was unfair to the other students who had complied to allow this student to pass or that I was rewarding a kid who had not put forth the necessary effort to be successful.

The decisions we face as educators can be quite complex and leave us feeling vulnerable. Sometimes we must be willing to stand up for what we believe is right and advocate for those who don't know how to advocate for themselves. The reason I struggled so much with this situation was because all I could think of was how that young boy reminded me of myself when I was in high school. I wanted him to know that I believed in him like Mr. Morgan believed in me. He simply needed a champion. The kind of champion I had in Mr. Morgan, without whom I would never have graduated from high school, much less gone on to become a teacher or school administrator.

As teachers we need to push kids to learn at high levels. We must not be afraid to make exceptions for some kids who may need extra time or extra help to complete the required work. Whatever you do, hold them accountable for learning and don't allow students to submit work that is not of high quality. If we had done a better job of working with this student, his parents, and one another, we might have better understood why he didn't do the work or why his work reflected a lack of understanding of the content. Knowing this, we could have put the necessary support systems in place to make sure he completed the required work at a level that accurately demonstrated his learning. Being willing to treat kids differently does not negate the demand for high standards. It simply means that we are willing to recognize that different students have different needs, and it is okay to treat them accordingly.

Compelled to Share

When I was in fifth grade, I had a homework assignment to read a book in language arts class and write a five-hundred-word book report. To this day, I cannot remember the name of the book, but what I do recall is that I didn't read it. It wasn't that I didn't try to read it; I had difficulty sitting down or staying focused for any length of time back then. I came up with every excuse I could think of to avoid reading it. And writing? Well that was always a painful experience to the point I would cry. I knew I just couldn't write well.

The night before the book report was due, I went into my mom's bedroom and told her that I had finished reading the book and needed help writing my report. I remember her asking me questions about the book, specifically what the book was about and about some of the characters in it. I struggled to make something up, so I told her I wasn't feeling well and asked her if I could stay home the next day rather than go to school. My mother, being the smart woman she was, responded, "Yes," and then told me to go get ready for bed. I felt so relieved that I would have the entire next day to come up with something to write. As I walked toward the door, my mother's voice stopped me: "I will take your report to your teacher tomorrow once you finish it." I slowly walked to my room, laid down, and began to cry. A few moments later my mom walked into the room. "You didn't read the book, did you *mijo*?" she asked. "No, mommy," I responded. "I don't like to read, and you know I can't write." She leaned over and gave me a big hug and told me not to worry. "Someday you will be a great writer," she said in a quiet voice, "someday."

From the outside, it may appear that I actually enjoy writing. After all, I have already co-authored two books, and here I sit trying to accomplish it once again, this time on my own. Well, the truth is, I don't. I lost confidence in my reading and writing way back in elementary school, and I still struggle to write today. In fact, struggle may be too soft a word to describe it. It's more like I agonize over it. I literally freeze up and can find myself spending hours sitting and producing nothing. Like many of our students whom we have identified as "slow" or reluctant learners who continue to struggle in the areas of reading and writing, I often feel like giving up whenever I sit down to write. For years I lacked the necessary skills to read at high levels or write at a proficient level due to gaps in my learning. Likewise, many students carry this heavy burden throughout their schooling. They are then placed into remedial programs, or in some cases are even denied the opportunity to join their peers in traditional language arts courses. This is because we have been led to believe that a student who is reading four, five, or even six grade levels below where they should be cannot do grade-level course work. On the contrary, we must do everything we possibly can to ensure all students are receiving grade-level content while receiving the necessary one-on-one support to continue to grow and develop their literacy skills. A student who never receives grade-level content will never attain the level we all hope for them to achieve. This is because they are never exposed to, much less expected to learn, grade-level material. We instead relinquish them to another teacher, program, or classroom to work. I know this feeling all too well because that is what happened to me during my middle school years. Instead of receiving the proper support I needed to "catch up," I fell further and further behind as my skills continued to deteriorate. Unfortunately, this experience would continue to circle back throughout my schooling and into my adult life.

Admittedly, things did not change much throughout my school years. I avoided as much reading and writing as I could. With each successive writing assignment, I conned my way through most of it. Once in college, I knew that strategy would no longer work, so I tried a different approach: I sought out my professors and told them I wasn't a very good writer and that I feared my lack of writing skills would prevent me from being successful in the class. Although I made it through my classes, my confidence never increased.

Until six years ago, I can honestly say not much had changed regarding my feelings toward writing. The reading became more enjoyable, but the writing, well, let's just say I surrounded myself with good writers who could edit my work.

I have shared with others on many occasions that I credit George Couros (@gcouros) for encouraging me to share my voice through writing by blogging. Luckily for me, he didn't buy into any of the lame excuses I had used with my prior teachers, professors, and colleagues. Instead, he encouraged me, pushed me, and more importantly, convinced me that I could actually do it. "How can you expect others to do what you are not willing to do yourself?" asked George. "After all, aren't you the guy who always says, 'What we model is what we get?'" I knew he was right, and within a month, I gathered up the courage to post my first blog. Today, I am still going strong, but it doesn't mean I still don't relive those moments of self-doubt.

Who do I write for today? Well, I write for myself because I want to be a better writer and share my learning with others. I write for my children because I want to show them they can accomplish anything they set their minds to and that some of the greatest rewards in life come from persevering through difficult times. And finally, I write for my mother because I want her to be proud of me. It's one way to show my appreciation for her believing in me. I am not quite sure I will ever be the great writer she professed I would be, but I know she is proud of my work.

I often think about how our students feel when given a writing assignment. Do they receive the kind of patience, support, and encouragement needed to overcome their lack of confidence or moments of despair? And what about our teachers? Do they feel compelled to help but are overwhelmed with the number of students who come to them deficient in skills combined with the expectation to elevate those with advanced skills to even greater heights? What is important to remember is that working with all students, regardless of their level, takes time, patience, a positive attitude, and a certain level of persistence to inspire our children to believe they can do anything! Even our most talented students must work hard at their writing, and there will still be moments when self-doubt begins to creep in. It is in these moments, more than ever, that our children need a champion, regardless of their abilities, to push them forward. They need to know that we are by their side.

Be sure to share these helpful tips with your students or colleagues when it comes to writing:

- Start writing and keep writing your thoughts down on paper.

- Once you see your thoughts written down, you will be able to piece them together.

- Get the negative thoughts out of your mind and believe in yourself.

- Don't be afraid of what others will think; everyone has something to contribute.

- Forget about what it looks and sounds like. Just write.

- It only takes one person to relate to your story. Honor your impact.

- Embrace your vulnerability. Give of yourself and don't be afraid to share your story.

- Reach out to others whom you trust to "check you" back into perspective.

- It is normal to experience writer's block. It happens to everyone, even the best writers.

- Write for you. Reflection is powerful and necessary for individual growth.

So what can we take away from this, especially when we know we have students today sitting in our classrooms at every level from third grade to high school to college believing that they cannot write well? Over time they have managed to figure out ways to "get by" while not only lacking the necessary skills on how to write a quality paper, but also lacking the necessary confidence to do so. If we want students progressing through school year after year having developed the necessary writing skills to be successful students, then we must support classroom teachers by partnering with them to ensure we are providing all students with "real" writing experiences, not only at school but at home. We need to provide structure, specific strategies, quality feedback, direction, support, and modeling on a consistent basis. Strong writers are nurtured by adults who share quality examples, ask relevant and meaningful questions, accept different forms, provide a place and time to inspire personal written reflection, encourage collaboration, and of course, celebrate and honor their writing through publication or media of some sort. By adults personally investing in each child's writing, I believe students at all levels can shine and become great writers with you as their champion by their side.

Listen to Students

Whether it's during conversations or concerns regarding discipline, their choices or decisions, their role on a team or organization, or simply wanting to know how life is going, all children deserve to have the adults in their school community take time to listen to them when they have something to share. It's easy, though, to dismiss students' concerns about workloads or consequences as whining or complaining because, let's face it, sometimes kids complain. Listen to kids anyway, and even if it sounds like whining or complaining, resist the reflex to cut them off. (Let's be honest here: Sometimes we adults can be just as likely to complain when we don't like something. The first lesson here is to recognize that while we tend to be hypercritical of what we perceive as selfish behavior in our students, we need to keep our own complaints in check if we want people to listen to us.)

While you're listening to your students, be sure to ask clarifying questions to further understand their position. Through the years, I have learned to get better at asking relevant questions and, as a result, have been rewarded with kinder and more respectful responses from students (and adults, for that matter).

Once you understand the situation, your initial response may be to fix the problem. By nature, many of us went into education because we are *fixers*. We hear about someone's problem, and we immediately start trying to figure out how to fix it. One of the hardest things about being in a position to make decisions is that there are many problems we *can* fix and make the student happy—at least initially. But that doesn't mean taking over and providing the solution is the right thing to do or is even in the best or long-term interest of the student. Sometimes the hardest thing to do is to listen and learn more about the issue and then help the students come up with their own solutions.

ARM Yourself for Tough Conversations

Not fixing an issue for someone can be a difficult choice, especially when we know that harsh feelings are sure to follow, either from the student or even a parent. Sometimes you know going into a conversation that the person with the need or complaint will have to take responsibility to fix the problem. You are simply there to be the sounding board or perhaps provide direction. When I know I'm heading into a tough conversation with someone (a student, parent, or even a colleague) who wants me to fix something, I ARM myself. No, not that type of arming. ARMing myself for a difficult conversation equips me to be strategic in my thoughts, decisions, and actions. It is not about being manipulative; it is about being mindful not to minimize the impact my response could have on others. Thinking ahead gives me a tactical advantage as I determine and plan for a critical conversation. It also allows me to consider how I can create an environment where people feel listened to and validated.

I try to never walk into a situation "unARMed," or in other words, not having taken the time to think through a scenario which could have the potential to unravel or have a negative outcome. Here's what it means to ARM yourself:

- **Acknowledge—Successful people enter every conversation focused on the other person.** Recognize that relationships with others are the most important factor in cultivating a culture of trust and influence. Invest your time, energy, and concern in an empathetic way. Approach each situation with an understanding that at the heart of every problem is a conversation to be had. You must be prepared for the reality that your best attempts at acknowledging someone else's feelings or position won't always produce the results you had hoped. Even so, you can find solace in knowing that you were intentional and sincere in your efforts.

> ## Approach each situation with an understanding that at the heart of every problem is a conversation to be had.

- **Rectify—Strong teachers and leaders recognize that it is possible to stay calm and rationally seek solutions even in the midst of chaos.** Communicate and model the importance of rectifying the dilemma—addressing the issue, not simply the symptoms—with the available resources. Rather than taking on more work for yourself by fixing a problem for someone, help the person find ways to make the best of the situation. Be supportive, regardless of your role in the process, but also be willing to accept that not every problem is yours to "fix."

- **Move On—Effective teachers and leaders have a unique ability to accept their circumstances and move on rather than spend time and energy dwelling on things that are beyond their control.** If you have played a part in creating the problem, it is crucial that you quickly take responsibility by admitting your role and apologizing for your error, then move into solution mode. Remember, the most effective educators don't stigmatize mistakes made by themselves or others, because doing so creates a culture where students and staff members fear making mistakes. Failure is often the first ingredient in the recipe for success. No educator is immune from complex situations. The best teachers and leaders know that, while it's possible to exhaust every moment in a quest to support their students and colleagues alike in their learning, they must learn to reflect on each experience in a strategic way to improve their chances for future success.

Address the Barriers to a Culture Focused on Championing for Students

So how do these fundamental core elements—taking time to personally search out students, engaging them in conversations (both meaningful and frivolous), and genuinely listening to them—so often go ignored in schools? It could be an intentional decision or an unintentional oversight. Regardless, it's a problem—a mindset—that must be corrected if we're going to improve the culture of our schools. Let me offer a few reasons why I believe this issue of disengagement and personal investment continues to exist in schools across the country and what we can do as teachers and leaders to address it:

"There isn't time." I get it; we're all busy. Even so, it is imperative that we intentionally create opportunities to spend time with students. I believe that every adult at a school should strive to connect with students. I also know that schools everywhere have staff members who *want* to spend more time with students. So, at a minimum, let's get those teachers and administrators working together to carve out time for students and staff to talk with and learn from one another. It's a matter of trading time. Take inventory of where you are not being efficient with your time (meetings come to mind; limit them to one hour) and begin putting processes into place that result in more efficient use of your time.

"It's not my job." To the contrary, there is no element more critical for school success than for a staff to believe and behave in a manner that models a student-first mindset. This kind of culture starts with the building leader and teachers creating a common vision and agreeing upon values that honor every student. This is done by holding educators accountable for delivering quality content in meaningful ways *and* cultivating positive, personal relationships with students. Every staff member needs to remember that students are our most precious commodity. Without them, we don't have a job. We may not want to forget that critical piece of information (as a smile spreads across my face), right?

> **Every staff member needs to remember that students are our most precious commodity. Without them, we don't have a job.**

"Dealing with challenges isn't worth the potential negative response." Teachers and building leaders must be prepared to support one another during challenging times with students and their parents. We must recognize we won't always get it right and that our best chance for success comes from working through difficult moments together with a non-critical eye, protecting each other rather than placing blame when we don't achieve the desired outcome. Taking time to walk through anticipated responses from each other ahead of time can help everyone avoid potential pitfalls. Success often comes down to each individual acting with courage and engaging in tough conversations.

"When students behave poorly or fail to do the work, they don't deserve my time or attention." This thought won't enter your mind if you recognize that we work with children/young adults who in most cases have not developed the ability to think beyond the short term. In most cases they simply do not have the experience or level of maturity to understand the long-term consequences of their choices or actions. It is imperative that we don't make their behavior about us. Our focus must always be on the learning opportunities that lie before us, not just for the student but for us as well.

We can't expect that our students will always have opinions that coincide with the way we see things in our adult world. But we can expect they will have experiences as students that will shape them, and it is our responsibility as the adults to set the tone for those experiences and make sure we never leave a student asking, "Why won't he or she just listen to me?"

Never underestimate the impact that purposeful and positive engagement with students can have on a school community. And never pass up an opportunity to smile and greet a student in a positive way. After all, students are inherently the most important people entering our school building. One of my mentors shared this poem with me early on in my role as principal. It became the mantra that drove much of our work as an administrative team. It's entitled, *Take Care of the Student*:

*Students are the most important people
entering our facilities.*

*Students are not an interruption of our work;
they are the purpose of it.*

*We are not doing them a favor by serving them.
They are entitled to our service.*

*Students are not cold statistics; they are human
beings with feelings and emotions like our own.*

*Students are people who bring us their wants,
and it is our job to handle them as
expeditiously as possible.*

Take care of the student; that's why we are here.

—Author Unknown

> **Students are inherently
> the most important people
> entering our school building.**

Many schools today have a *can't-do* culture. If adults buy into the mindset that kids can't, then how can we complain when kids won't? Every day, students are being reminded to follow the rules, do as you're told, get in line, wait your turn, raise your hand, stop talking, don't do that, etc. We need to shift this practice and strive to culturize a school where students are encouraged to do what's not allowed by giving them permission to do what was previously seen as not possible based on policy or regulations. By being intentional in our interactions with students and learning to understand and appreciate their goals and aspirations, we will come to recognize the accomplishments of students who have overcome adversity and personal challenges to reach their full potential in school—in academics, attendance, behavior, or overall citizenship.

If adults buy into the mindset that kids can't, then how can we complain when kids won't?

When we take time to acknowledge their contributions, we also find that behind every student success story is a staff member who championed for that student. Look at the comments shared with me by a student about one her teachers. As you read it, you'll see that "Mrs. F." is a model of what it means to be a champion for students.

Behind every student success story is a staff member who championed for that student.

Mrs. F knows my high school trauma story and assures me every day she is here to help make school as easy as possible for me. With the push and drive she gives me, I know I have enough support to stay in school. Mrs. F not only cares for me as a student, she cares for me as a person. I know when I feel like things are impossible to get done, Mrs. F reminds me to not give up. Any dream can be achieved, even when you have the responsibility of raising a two-year-old child. I had planned to drop out of school again, but did not let anyone know because I knew they would try to discourage me. After talking to Mrs. F regarding my future plans for a nursing career, I realized dropping out was not the way to go. It seemed as if every time I was down in the dumps or upset, Mrs. F would find a way to make me smile, even if it meant leaving a friendly note on an assignment. I know if I had not met Mrs. F, I probably would have dropped out of school again. I love Mrs. F dearly, and though I am losing her as a teacher, I hope and know I will always have her as a friend.

By taking time to actively engage our students in conversation, we are opening up treasure chests filled with testimonials from students who have persevered through difficult family situations, overcome personal tragedies, suffered through times of poor performance in school or struggled with severe learning disabilities. We become privy to stories of students who have defeated personal substance abuse issues, overcome expulsions from school, suffered severe brain injuries, struggled with personal health issues, or defeated cancer. All these students demonstrate a certain degree of resiliency with the courage to keep fighting. Their stories inspire us and allow us, as educators, to remember that our work matters—that connecting with and championing for students matters more than we may ever know. In a culture of excellence, every student has at least one adult to whom he or she can go for encouragement or support in their time of need. Will you be the one?

CHAMPION FOR STUDENTS

Within the heart of every caring educator is the core belief that students are worth the time and energy it takes to establish relationships with them. In many cases, it is a personal investment and commitment from an adult to a student that results in the student experiencing success and ultimately graduating. It isn't always easy, but it is worth it.

To close out this chapter, I want to offer you three culture-building ideas that you can put into practice right away. They are mindsets and actions that will help you make a greater difference in the life of your students:

CULTURE BUILDER #1

Recognize What's Going Well—As a classroom teacher, take a moment to reflect on the work you do with students. If you are in a school or district leadership position, ask your staff members to reflect on their work with students and what they do to cultivate a positive culture in their classrooms. One school administrator I know was generally moved by the responses her teachers gave as they described the ways they worked to create a positive culture of learning in their classrooms. She was so proud of her team and inspired by the list of ideas they shared that she decided to share the responses with her entire faculty during a professional-development activity. She did this to remind her staff that they are the silver bullet in education. Here is the question she posed:

Please share a strategy you use to illuminate a culture of learning in your classroom and share your belief in why it matters.

CULTURE BUILDER #2

Change Student Behavior by Changing Adult Behavior—We get what we model. One area in which this reality is blatantly obvious is in regard to referrals. Across the nation, teachers and administrators continually look for solutions for reducing student behavior referrals. Behavioral tools and programs across the country are infiltrating our buildings as school leaders search for the silver bullet to this issue. No matter what program your school implements, the first step toward making significant improvements in student behavior is to recognize that the adults in your organization are the silver bullet. In other words, if you want to improve student behavior in your school, you must change the way the adults in your school interact with students and with each other.

Take time to review the archives of referrals that have accumulated during the past year and ask yourself this question: "How many of the referrals that were written by staff members originated with a comment, response, interaction, behavior, or in some cases, a lack of response that, rather than de-escalate a situation, actually served to provoke a student, resulting in a behavioral referral to the office? What you may find is that many of the student referrals were written when a teacher felt exacerbated or frustrated with a student. We've all been there. We allow a student to push our buttons and then we respond in a way that is out of character for us. Why? Because we care so darn much.

Even if the adults in your organization handle situations superbly, some student situations will still result in referrals. When that happens, flip your mindset and view the interaction as an opportunity to cultivate a relationship with a student who needs you in their corner.

CULTURE BUILDER #3

Reach Out and Call Someone—Devote time regularly to contacting families whose students are struggling with attendance. If you are a school leader, make sure to provide some time during the school hours (an early release or late arrival day or a specific time on a professional development day) for your staff to make those calls. One great practice is to meet and share the results of those conversations with one another.

Evidence is clear that students who have a history of poor attendance also do poorly in school, are disconnected, and ultimately are highly at risk for dropping out of school. Personal phone calls, letters, home visits, delegating local resources, such as school counselors, nurses, social workers, school resource officers, etc.—if done with the intention of better understanding the struggles your students and their families are facing—can make a significant impact on a student's desire to attend school. Sometimes all it takes to establish a personal connection is for someone to reach out and say, "We care, and we are here to support you and your family." That one interaction may well change a student's or parent's attitude about school. In the more serious situations, we can reach out to local agencies, such as the Department of Human Services, Juvenile Court, Police Department, etc. for assistance in supporting the student in a positive way, socially, emotionally, and academically. The key is to keep trying and never give up on a child or a family, to commit to doing whatever it takes to create a plan that ensures any child can and will be successful. Believing is half the battle, but believing must be followed up with actions to complete the other half.

Educators around the world are transforming their classrooms and schools by being intentional in their daily interactions with students, colleagues, and families. They recognize that it begins with them and that the most important factor in determining the success or failure of any student is the way they connect with students on a level whereby the student believes that the adults care about them personally. They have learned that when it comes to building positive relationships with others, how they respond is their choice. They don't put the onus on others; rather, they place it on themselves. Culture builders understand that the promise of expectations left unfulfilled can sometimes leave them feeling drained and defeated, resulting in disappointment and heartache; however, they never lose hope. They understand that often their students are inhibited by the three Cs, but with patience and unwavering support, their students can overcome these moments of adversity and persevere. They also remain committed to the idea that fair sometimes means treating students differently in order to level the playing field for some. The fact is, some kids just take longer to demonstrate learning, just like some adults. Those who believe this also believe that students are our most precious commodity. Behind every child's face is a story that needs to be heard, appreciated, respected, valued, and in some cases, shared. Educators who champion for students have a sincere desire to create positive experiences for their students and others that will motivate and inspire them to be the change our schools and communities need!

We need you to be that change. The kind of change that when you look into the eyes of a student whose inner voice is saying, "I don't think I can do this," your eyes, your voice, your actions, say, "Yes you can!" By consistently interacting and connecting in a purposeful manner with your students, you can reawaken their spirit and influence them in meaningful ways that will instill a sense of belonging and a belief that they have something positive to contribute.

QUESTIONS FOR DISCUSSION

» To transform teaching and learning, we must first transform our belief systems. In what ways are you (or could you be) the silver bullet for your students or staff?

» When was the last time you advocated for a student? What was the result? What are some other ways to proactively address common struggles to turn them into victories?

» We know that many students struggle in school due to the 3 Cs: They don't feel connected, they don't feel capable, and they lack confidence. How can we effectively engage students so they don't feel this way?

» In what ways can we personally invest in our students and each other so every member of a school community feels like they have a personal champion?

CHAPTER 3

CORE PRINCIPLE 2:
Expect Excellence

*A leader's most powerful ally
is his or her own example.*

—John Wooden

A **few years ago, I met with a special young man who had been dropped from school several times due to non-attendance.** His name was Ben. One day, Ben stopped by school to visit with his English teacher, a gentleman he trusted and respected. After a heart-to-heart chat, the teacher encouraged Ben to come see me and told him I would treat him fairly. He also reminded him his graduation window was closing, and he needed to follow through this time on his promise to commit to school, attend regularly, and do what was expected of him if he wanted to earn his diploma. Nineteen years old and closing in on twenty, Ben begged me for one last chance to earn his high school diploma. Ben had a history of making poor decisions and, quite frankly, for making promises and then not delivering on those promises. This time he vowed it would be different.

"Why is this time going to be different than the previous times," I asked? "Because it is my last chance and I don't want to be a dropout!" he exclaimed. This time I could sense a desperation, a different level of urgency in his voice. "Do you understand you have to go the entire year and pass every class to earn every credit to graduate?" I asked. "Yes, I do! Please Mr. Casas, I promise I won't let you down," Ben said. Considering his promise, I reached into my desk drawer and pulled out a pen and a piece of paper and handed it to him. "I want it in writing. You better not let me down, Ben. You know why? Because you are not going to be the last Ben that comes to me wanting another chance, and I need for you to give me hope to keep believing in kids when they come back asking for second and third chances," I said. As he walked out of my office, I unfolded the piece of paper he had left on my desk. It read, "I promise I won't let you down Mr. Casas. Consider this an invitation to my graduation party."

That May, I smiled and got teary-eyed as I read Ben's name at graduation. Just two months prior, we had recognized Ben at an awards banquet for overcoming adversity and persevering through difficult times. That evening he read a letter he had written that included many touching comments about our staff and me. I couldn't help but get choked up as I talked about him at the banquet. That afternoon after the graduation ceremony, I was the first one to show up at Ben's home with card in hand. As he opened up the card, a big smile came over his face. Inside his graduation card I had placed the note he had written that past fall promising me he would not let me down. In his card I simply wrote, "Thanks for giving me hope to continue believing in the Bens of the world." With that, he gave me a huge hug and thanked me for believing in him.

The truth was, it is I who owed Ben the biggest thanks of all for showing me the importance of not only seeing the best in all kids but *expecting* the best from all kids.

Expecting excellence, our second core principle, is essential when it comes to fostering a culture in which one's best effort is the standard, and everyone in the school community is a leader.

Leaders Don't Need a Title

One of my favorite movies of all time is *A Few Good Men*, released in 1992, starring Tom Cruise, Jack Nicholson, Demi Moore, and Kevin Bacon. I have watched the movie dozens of times, and each time I can't help but recite the lines along with the characters. One line at the end of the movie always makes me think about our work in schools: "Harold, you don't need to wear a patch on your arm to have honor." Those words, spoken by Cruise's character, Lieutenant Kafee, strike a chord with me. I think that is because of the way I view leadership. You don't have to have a leadership title to be a leader. You just have to lead. When you have a disposition about you that others immediately recognize and sometimes want to emulate, you are a leader. When you draw people in and make them want to be around you, you are a leader. Maybe you have a unique skill set that people quickly notice and appreciate, or maybe it's your words or tendency to notice the best in others that inspires the people around you to want to be better. Even if you aren't privileged with a reserved parking space or a nameplate on your desk, you simply go about your daily work, serving as an ambassador to your community. Perhaps it's as an unofficial mentor to a co-worker or a positive role model to your student. Maybe it's by taking great pride in and caring deeply about your school community. That's what makes you a leader.

Throughout my career, I have been blessed with the good fortune of working with incredibly talented and dedicated teachers. One morning I was sitting at an interview table with my instructional coaches discussing potential teacher candidates, and the conversation came around to what it meant to be a "model" teacher. Of course, the movie *A Few Good Men* came up. (Ok, I'm probably the one who brought it up.) Just as in leadership, we agreed, teachers don't need a special title (e.g., instructional coach, curriculum coordinator, team leader, etc.) to be a model to their students or their colleagues. As the discussion continued, I thought about the level of excellence of the teachers and leaders who surrounded me and wondered what it was that made them "model" teachers and leaders. In considering their attributes, here are the commonalities I noticed:

- They recognized they were a work in progress. They didn't consider themselves "experts" and valued the importance of learning from others.

- They didn't define themselves as "model" teachers/leaders; they defined themselves as model *learners*.

- They never kept their heads down or "stayed in their lane" when it came to leading. They instead chose to push themselves forward in order to disrupt the status quo to bring about positive change for students, their school, and their community.

- They visualized the change they wanted for their schools. They understood that how they thought and what they believed could impact what their students and school could become.

- They didn't shy away from challenges and never took a defeatist attitude. They stayed the course regardless of the arrows that may have come their way.

- They didn't expect everything to go as planned. They recognized that working in schools with kids was unpredictable. They saw student discipline issues as opportunities to both learn and teach self-discipline.

- When faced with adversity, they didn't dwell on the negative; they approached it as an opportunity to educate others.

- They were mindful that how they modeled teaching and/or leading each day was a choice, and they chose to bring their best each day, and the next day, and the day after that.

After we were done discussing our candidates that day, I couldn't help but feel proud of the people who sat at the table with me. As a building leader, I knew I demanded a lot of my support staff, teachers, instructional coaches, and administrative team, and they met the challenge.

As leaders, I think we must invest every fiber of our belief and energy to help those we serve develop confidence and skills so they can realize that leaders don't need a patch, badge, title, or nameplate to be considered a model teacher or a leader. It's the way we manage ourselves every day that allows us the privilege of leadership in whatever position we hold.

Leaders Build Capacity

Everyone in an organization has the fundamental capacity to lead. Yes, everyone. That includes teachers, students, counselors, nurses, assistant principals, para-professionals, directors, and so on—without exception.

Whenever I bring up the topic of leadership in conversation, I find it interesting that so many people immediately respond by telling me they have no desire to be a principal or school administrator. I then remind them of the previous point: Just because you are not the building principal doesn't mean you don't have the skills to lead others, whether they be students, colleagues, or in some instances, the administration. In fact, I see this kind of leadership all the time. Talented teachers take it upon themselves to do all they can to see that each of their students, as well as the school in general, experiences success. They may do this by serving on committees, volunteering as mentors, representing the school at a community event, presenting on a topic at a board meeting, or partnering with colleagues to write curriculum. These teachers stand outside their doorway and greet students, they contact parents on a regular basis, sit toward the front at faculty meetings, stop by the main office to thank the secretaries, and support their colleagues by sharing their best lessons. They genuinely want to help others around them move forward and experience their own successes.

As stated in the previous section, you don't need to have the title of "principal" to be a leader. You are a leader because of your ability to inspire others, to build their confidence, to influence their thinking and, more importantly, their behavior. And as you do so, you develop new leaders. In fact, helping others increase their capacity and develop their leadership skills—at the student, teacher, building, and district level—is our fundamental responsibility as educators. Building a community of leaders is how we create school cultures where everyone, from the youngest student to the most seasoned educator, believes they have an obligation to be a *culturizer* with the power to impact the school in a positive way.

The most effective leaders are always learning and are willing to share their expertise in hopes that someone will benefit in some way.

They have figured out that leadership was not meant to be a committee of one, exercised in isolation. No one person was ever meant to lead a classroom, school, or district all alone, not if they want to propel the work that needs to be done to a maximum level of efficiency and to sustain a high quality of work over a long period of time. Over the years I have encountered many teachers and administrators who admittedly believed they had to be the sole leader when they first took over a classroom or building. Most felt they had the passion, drive, energy, and work ethic to manage and lead their students or teachers all by themselves, and for a few years they may have been somewhat successful. What they soon realized, however, is that they could be much more effective and efficient if they cultivated more leaders: Leaders who would support the classroom expectations or the school's mission and vision by trusting their students or their staff and putting them in a position to use their skills, talents, strengths, and voices.

If students or staff members are constantly asking for permission, you have not done a very good job of building capacity. If that's currently true for you as a classroom teacher or a building or district leader, understand you will never reach the level of excellence your students and staff deserve. An organization that is always seeking

> **If students or staff members are constantly asking for permission, you have not done a very good job of building capacity.**

permission has not generated the capacity or developed the leadership skills that empower everyone to work toward the common goal of excellence using their unique skills, traits, and talents. If you're stuck in the "permission" trap, either with your students or your staff members, you can begin to change that today by creating a framework based on a clearly defined set of core values or a belief system. Those values will drive the decisions and behaviors of those in your organization, and the framework will give others appropriate responsibilities and empower them to develop their own leadership skills.

Leaders Do the Simple Things

I feel confident that most people who are not in the education profession would marvel at the number of interactions and conversations school teachers and leaders have on a daily basis. I am comfortable estimating that number to be in the hundreds—sometimes by lunch time. It is this part of the work that most of us enjoy and value above all our other responsibilities. Perhaps that's because we know that by investing time and energy in others, even through the simplest of interactions, we can play a part in helping them become better. And at the same time, *we* become better.

Throughout your life, you have probably experienced a wide range of personal interactions with educators as well as non-educators who have helped shape you as a teacher and/or leader. More importantly, they helped shape you as a person. If you're like me, you have people in your life who regularly push your thinking, force you to pause and reflect, and gently remind you of your ability to influence others. I hope you'll allow me, at least for a moment, to be one of those people. Here are some simple thoughts that I hope will cause you to pause, think, and act.

- **Embrace your vulnerability.** When did you last try something for the first time? We ask kids to put themselves out there every day, and we sometimes forget what it feels like to be completely vulnerable. Are you asking your students to do something that you are not willing to do?

- **Don't wait for others to do what needs to be done; do it yourself.** Want to build a community that currently doesn't exist? Take initiative and be the change you so desire to see happen. Take an idea and act! It's that simple.

- **Take time to enjoy what you do!** Sometimes we forget to take notice of the difference we are making in serving others. Celebrate your successes! When we focus our energy on giving of ourselves to others (and we take time to enjoy the process and the outcome), others notice the magnitude of our joy and passion to serve and become inspired to do the same.

- **If you want people to be less anxious, provide more clarity.** How often do we get frustrated with students or staff who we feel are not able to follow directions? When that happens, ask yourself, "Were the directions as clear as they could have been?" If not, own it, regroup, and try again, this time focusing on more specifics of what you want.

- **You are the difference between today and tomorrow.** Do you believe you can have a generational impact on families? It's true that *hope* is not a plan, but it is a beginning. Every success story begins when someone takes the vital first step to hope and believe that change is possible. Without hope, there is no plan. We all need someone to believe in us. Be that one!

- **Stay the course.** Stay focused on the long-term rather than short-term outcomes. We don't always get the benefit of seeing the immediate results of our work, but you can trust that others eventually will. And you can feel good knowing you played a part in your students' success.

- **Experience is still the best teacher.** If we believe this to be true, and if we want our students to truly find value in their experiences, then maybe we should put them in positions more often to experience failure—and the consequences that come with having failed. One of the best skills we can teach kids is failure recovery.

- **Build a résumé of failures.** Speaking of failure, every student should be required to submit their résumé of failures throughout their school experience and then share it for others to see. In fact, so should the adults. Failure should not be something that brings us shame; it helps us grow! We must teach and model to our students that failures don't have to equate to long-term doom; they benefit us by developing our grit, perseverance, and empathy when we commit to working through them. Learning from our "oops moments" allows us to value our accomplishments even more. Through this lens, even the smallest successes can be deeply admired.

Every day that we walk into our school, we are entrusted with the responsibility and gift of making a difference in our student's lives. We must be prepared to face the challenges, accept failures, honor successes, and take time to recognize that no single success or misstep is a final destination. As teachers and leaders, we serve as the barometer for our schools. By taking the time to listen and self-reflect on the words of others, we continue to shape our own inner core values and strengthen our belief system which guides us in our daily work with students and staff. If we want to change our relationships with others for the better, we must be willing to take the time to reflect and then change the way we manage those conversations and interactions. By doing so, we can leave a positive mark on those with whom we come in contact every day. It doesn't cost a penny to reach out and greet someone with a friendly smile, to strive to lift someone's spirit with a sincere compliment, support others with a heartfelt hug, or jolt those who are in dire straits with a blast of positive energy to help them get through the rest of the day. So what are you waiting for? All it takes is one simple interaction at a time to start a ripple effect that can transform someone's life forever.

It doesn't cost a penny to jolt those who are in dire straits with a blast of positive energy to help them get through the rest of the day.

Eyes on Culture
by Jennifer McDaniel
English teacher, Bettendorf High School, Bettendorf, Iowa

High expectations can be germinated and nurtured in a variety of places: home, school, peers, and self. But often the seeds are never planted. We know that true self-esteem comes not from pats on the back and generic praise but grows when a person is challenged beyond her natural limits and experiences success. It is our job then, as educators, to sow the seed when there is none, to water, to stake, and to shine on the seedling. It is important to set high expectations for ourselves and our students, but not if we are unwilling to take risks ourselves, not if we are unwilling to scaffold their learning with models, support, and patience, and not if we are unwilling to allow students to fail. Failure is often the best teacher because it fosters resilience, but we must provide the guidance and encouragement for students to be willing to try again.

I currently teach sophomore honors English, a class designed for students with reading scores in the seventy-fifth percentile or above. After the first week of introductions and skill review, we started to delve into more difficult analysis and writing when I noticed a student scanning the room with a bored, vacant look. Not surprisingly, she failed the first in-class essay, which prompted me to review her standardized test scores. She was in the forty-first percentile upon entering high school, and the fifty-first percentile upon entering sophomore year. In other words, she was in way over her head. After I talked to her and her counselor, I learned that failing honors English was the least of her problems. Her parents were divorced, and her mother made little time for her; she was struggling with depression and several other factors, but when given the opportunity to drop to general English, she said, "I don't want to. I am learning a lot from you." We worked together to outline the next in-class essay, on which she received a B. Then we worked together to outline her next formal paper. We wrote the first paragraph together, then she did the rest. Now after an assessment, she is the first in class to eagerly inquire, "Have you graded our quizzes yet?" I can watch her sprout and grow as she pushes herself to be successful because it feels good. I did not lower my expectations for her; I gave her the tools, support, and desire to climb to them."

Leaders Aren't Afraid to Say No

People often speculate why more people don't go into the role of administration. Reasons that are regularly tossed around include the long hours, the pressures of serving an entire community of people, standardized testing and strict accountability measures, federal mandates, dealing with difficult parents, and responding to school board members with personal agendas. In some districts, all these have proven to be true. But the one thing that leads to an enormous amount of pressure and stress is having to say "no" to people. Saying no has proven to be one of the most difficult tasks to which leaders are subjected. Despite the natural fear of disappointing people or dealing with negative reactions, saying no is unavoidable in the role of any leader.

Throughout my career as a building administrator, I kept a sign close by that read, "No Good Deed Goes Unpunished." That sign stood by me for twenty-two years, traveled to three different cities, and weathered countless looks from me after some very challenging conversations. That sign was a gift from my mentor, the principal who had given me my first assistant principal job. Those words of wisdom had carried me through many lonely moments and long nights when I stayed awake questioning my decisions. In later years, I would stare at the sign and reflect on the difficulties and challenges I faced early on in my career. One day I realized that many of the issues schools faced back in the 1990s are still hot buttons today: discipline, grades, personnel matters, playing time in sports, negative public perceptions, teacher retention, student and staff attendance, budget cuts, etc. In my moments of self-doubt, I had to remind myself of the tremendous opportunity every day to reinforce timeless life lessons related to these (and other issues) that, once learned, built character. One of the lessons I had to learn the hard way was the importance of saying no, even if saying yes felt easier and a lot less stressful. It took me years to learn and appreciate that, although gut wrenching at times, saying no was a skill I needed to develop if I was going to not only survive but thrive in my role as a leader. Here are a few things I have learned that may help you if you struggle with saying no:

1. **Pay attention to how you say no and what you do afterward.** In situations where you can anticipate an emotional reaction to a no response, pay closer attention to *how* you say no so it doesn't become more about you than the no itself. Regardless of how the message is received, take time to follow up with the individual or group whose request was denied. Doing so lets the other person or group know that you understand and respect their feelings of frustration and disappointment.

2. **Power and "rightness" aren't the same.** Holding the power to make the final decision doesn't mean you are always right. If you said no at first, but later see how the response could be a yes, don't let pride get in the way. It is important that you control your "emotional persistence" so that your need to be right doesn't jeopardize your credibility as a decision maker. My former colleague and current principal Joy Kelly (@joykelly05) would often say, "It is better to be kind than it is to be right."

3. **Accept that dealing with stressful situations is a part of saying no.** Expect some level of disappointment and frustration when your response to a request is not what the requestor hoped to receive. The way you handle these emotional encounters affects your personal stress level and will determine how you are perceived as a leader to your staff or a mentor for your students. Stress is an inherent part of an educator's work, but how you manage stress is up to you.

4. **Sometimes a no is the beginning of a deeper relationship.** I have been pleasantly surprised by the number of times that, after hitting me (verbally, not physically) with a negative reaction to a no, the disappointed party has come back later with an apology. It serves as a reminder that the relationships we form over time can become more deeply rooted if we manage ourselves appropriately when the initial reaction we receive to a no is harsh or hurtful.

Although there are moments when we all wish we could just say yes and avoid the stress that comes with a no, we must continue to remind ourselves of all the good that comes from doing the right thing as opposed to the easy thing. And if new information is presented that changes your initial response, that's okay. As with other areas of our work, taking time to reflect on our decisions as leaders, accepting that we don't always get things right, and then owning our mistakes are all valuable practices from which we can grow as we model them for others.

Leaders Don't Say "Gotcha!"

Over the past few years, thousands of social media users around the world have been sharing their one word for the year. Maybe you have seen these posts and been inspired by their selections of words, such as *empathy, attitude, kindness, purpose, resiliency, inspire, courage, engage, create, today,* and *balance* to name a few. Some may have selected their one word as part of a New Year's resolution or saw it as an opportunity to commit to a change in lifestyle. For others, maybe it was a chance to reflect and grow both personally and professionally.

As part of my New Year's resolution one year, I decided to embark on the challenge of selecting my one word for the New Year. I will admit I struggled to settle on just one word. I narrowed it down to two, one of which embodied the spirit I wanted to model to school leaders. The other bordered on how we as educators should never behave, especially if we aspire to develop a vibrant and healthy school culture. To me, the words were coupled in such a way that others may not have understood or appreciated their potential impact on another person or organization. So, I selected the first for my one word: *forgiveness.*

I initially focused on my need to forgive those who I believed had wronged me in some capacity. I quickly discerned that my focus needed to expand beyond my own willingness to forgive others. After all, wouldn't I be more fulfilled if I took it a step further and asked others for their forgiveness?

In my head, it seemed so.

As I focused on the various aspects of forgiveness, the other word continued to weigh on my mind. If you have ever been on the receiving end of this word, I think you will be able to relate to what I am about to share. It is a word that rips at our inner core and makes us question our commitment, loyalty, and value. What is this one word?

Gotcha!

Sadly, it is a word (or sentiment) I used too frequently during my early years as a teacher and again as an administrator. In my head, the "gotcha" was justified. I convinced myself that both students and staff got what they had coming to them. And if I felt a student or staff member had betrayed me in any way, I had every right to play the gotcha game right back. How terribly wrong I was to behave in such a manner!

I know I don't have the monopoly on how to lead, but I have learned through the years that great teaching and leading requires taking time for reflection and developing both a personal and professional mindset. And doing so demands being willing to change as necessary. Whatever position we hold, it is our responsibility not to culturize our schools with toxic gotcha moments, because doing so destroys the fiber of our communities.

What does a culture of gotcha do to students and staff?

- It makes them feel betrayed, devalued, disrespected, and in many cases, embarrassed.

- It causes individuals to believe the environment is set up to fail them.

- It designs a focus on placing blame rather than giving credit.

- It spawns an opportunity to tear down and discredit members of the organization rather than build them up.

- It shapes members to feel powerless and to believe that they lack the ability to influence change for the better.

- It produces an environment where opinions don't matter. If people try to explain or respond, their voice goes unheeded.

- It calls the integrity of its members into question and makes people feel that others cannot be trusted.

- It makes expectations from superiors unclear. People are left to try to figure out what their leader/teacher wants and then get nailed when they don't do what they are "supposed" to be doing.

- It creates an environment where members feel they can't take risks.

Even as I review this list now, I can remember mistakes I've made in my career. I also know that I need to heed my own advice and model forgiveness—forgiving myself for any poor choices I made and, if I haven't already done so, asking for forgiveness from those whom I may have wronged.

Ultimately, I decided that gotcha didn't have to be the one word I avoided. Instead, I decided to redefine gotcha to a positive term by spending more time trying to catch others doing something right. I embraced this one word as a way to celebrate the success of others when I caught them modeling excellence.

Eyes on Culture by Joy Kelly
Principal, Bettendorf High School, Bettendorf, Iowa

People often interchange the words excellence and perfection. In fact, excellence is from the Latin excellere, meaning "to surpass or excel." Expecting excellence from students or staff does not equate to expecting perfection. What a relief! I believe the most significant way adults at school can surpass ordinary school standards and excel in a manner that benefits all students rests in their willingness and ability to be reliable. Some of the most challenging behaviors students present at school are rooted in their experience of other adults letting them down, lashing out at them, and modeling poor emotional regulation.

A school's culture of excellence begins in the attendance office. When arriving at school (especially when late), students do not need the adults sounding harsh, annoyed, or judgmental. If we are observant, the body language and demeanor reveals the kind of start students have had to their day. Be a reliable adult by being pleasant, telling students you are happy to see them, and asking how you can help them have a successful day at school.

Reliable adults caringly hold students accountable by having high expectations for them and their behavior. They believe every student belongs in their classroom or at their school and every student will personally benefit by enrolling in their class or school. They consistently provide comfort and care to students, whether they are behaving the way the adult wishes them to behave or not. They demonstrate the kind of

> maturity necessary to avoid taking things personally. They seek clarification rather than make assumptions about the intentions or behaviors of their students. They are respectful. They know that the louder students swear or scream, the quieter and more empathetic the adults need to get. They know the more disrespectful a student is, the greater respect our words and actions must demonstrate. They model forgiveness and patience. They say, "I am sorry." They ask students, "What do you need me to better understand?" When reliable adults do and say what they should, students will excel in and out of the classroom."

Leaders Don't Shy Away from Push Back

One of the many blessings for which I am genuinely grateful is my position as an adjunct professor for Drake University. Like many who have left the classroom, it serves as an opportunity to impact the lives of others in a positive way and hopefully inspire students, regardless of the level of their educational experience, to aspire for greatness. As every teacher will tell you, there is no greater feeling than having a student sincerely thank you for being their teacher or, in this case, professor.

During one semester, one of my graduate students submitted an assignment that included a quote by Ohio State football coach Urban Meyer that got me thinking. In his book *Above the Line,* Coach Meyer stated the following: "How you feel is not the best guide for what you should do... press pause and ask yourself what this situation requires of you." I went back and read the quote again—and then again. I reflected on how this advice relates to the work we do as classroom and school or district leaders, and thoughts about my peers' and my experiences flooded my mind. A few days later, a good principal friend of mine reached out to me and a few others who serve in leadership roles to share a work-related issue that was weighing heavily on his mind. The immediate, encouraging, and insightful responses he received from his network of colleagues reminded me that, regardless of the emotional and stressful firestorms we sometimes must extinguish as teachers and leaders, we will come out stronger and wiser having lived through them.

Veteran educators are some of the most durable people I know. They are amazingly adept at handling the emotional toll and stress that comes with teaching and leading schools. Why? For one, *they must be* to survive the pressures that come with the volume of decisions they need to make on any given day. Secondly, they are aware of the weight their decisions carry and, over time, get accustomed to being on the receiving end of an abundance of emotion. Without a strong sense of self-awareness and self-confidence, those stressful encounters could leave them feeling inept (and sometimes that feeling creeps in despite their experience). The third, and perhaps the most distressing, is that they may have had to learn to navigate the ego and personal, self-serving agendas of those who oppose their decisions. Obviously, not all opposition is bad, but too often the motives of competent educators get called into question when they run contrary to a parent's or colleague's wishes.

Being a classroom, school, or district leader today requires a great deal of fortitude, especially for those who aim to influence the status quo. Push back is to be expected, which means that having the courage to see things through is necessary in the work you do, especially when you see it through the eyes of your students. Below are just a few of the ways or areas in which a school leader's resolve might be tested:

1. **Hiring.** Building principals must communicate to their staff that they will make the final decision on all new hires. That is not to negate the value of having a team to help in the process, but everyone must be clear about their role in the decision-making process. It is imperative that principals invest time in this process. Hiring the best people is the most important responsibility school leaders have, yet it often remains the area in which we invest the least amount.

2. **Teacher Changes.** When a parent's request for a different teacher for their child is not granted, the emotionally charged issue can quickly go south. It is the leader's responsibility to implement a process for addressing these requests that is equitable for all kids and fair to all teachers. All teachers deserve an opportunity to address any concerns from parents first. Teacher changes should only be granted after attempts to resolve the concerns with the student, parent, teacher, and administrator have been unsuccessful.

3. **Suspensions.** Sometimes removal of students is necessary to ensure the safety of others. But supporting students in acquiring the necessary skills to help them manage themselves better takes time, patience, and intentional interventions. Interventions, such as behavioral modules, must provide students with opportunities to reflect on their decisions/behaviors and provide a platform for dialogue and mediation with adult guidance to impact change over time. Unfortunately, most suspensions that are appealed happen in the athletic arena, which often sends mixed messages to students and the community about the importance and value placed on sports over teaching honesty, integrity, and character.

4. **Technology/Social Media.** I think it's time that educators and parents alike recognize that the world as we knew it changed in the early nineties with the birth of the World Wide Web. There is no going back; 24/7 access to information and global connections are here to stay. Let's embrace this new reality and work on how to better leverage technology tools to create more invigorating, authentic, and connected learning experiences for students, parents, teachers, and schools alike. Let's stop placing blame on devices for all that is wrong with learning in schools today and start expecting more of ourselves as the leaders. Let's work together to figure out a solution.

5. **Internal Candidates.** Whom to choose? This is one of the most grueling of all tasks because, regardless of which internal candidate you choose, you know someone is going to be left devastated by your selection. The fallout from a wounded staff member can also leave a sour taste with colleagues who supported this staff member's desire for a new position, and serious push back can ensue. If you are not completely transparent from the onset or if you fail to respond appropriately to these emotionally charged situations, your credibility may be damaged long term. If you don't believe an individual is qualified enough to be seriously considered, don't play a game and make that person go through the application/interview process. Although it's difficult, the right thing to do is sit down and be honest about where you see this hopeful person fitting in long term. How an employee manages themselves during this conversation will tell you whether you made the right decision.

6. **New Initiatives.** Leaders create a path for change, and part of that responsibility is about mindset. We need to move beyond the rhetoric that change is difficult. As educators, we do ourselves a disservice when we continue to reinforce and perpetuate that belief. Change is not always difficult. It is not always scary. In fact, *not* changing is scary. Becoming irrelevant is scary. I have learned over the years that it is not change that gets most teachers and administrators worked up. Instead, what teachers fear is not having the time necessary to change or the support or the resources to help support the change. That fear can lead to a defeatist attitude rather than a winning attitude. We need to begin to see change as exhilarating, exciting, beneficial, and necessary to grow and develop our craft. As leaders, we need to do a better job of focusing on less and doing it better while providing more time and the right support for our teachers.

The inventory of feelings that many school leaders experience regularly would require an immediate check-in at an employee-assistance program in many other professions. Knowing where to expect push back and then preparing mentally and emotionally for it empowers leaders to be durable and agile. And even if, at times, your mental fortitude is challenged to the maximum level, regardless of how you feel, remember you can press pause and ask yourself what the situation requires. You cannot avoid the inevitable push back that comes from making decisions, but how you respond to it will determine your credibility and success as a school leader. After all, leadership is not just about how we behave when we know what to do; rather, it is best seen in the actions we take when we don't know what to do.

> **Leadership is not just about how we behave when we know what to do; rather, it is best seen in the actions we take when we don't know what to do.**

Leaders Value Communication

Many of the issues I see schools facing today are deeply embedded in how people communicate, neglect to communicate in a timely fashion, or in some instances, fail to communicate all together. My experience has been that most of the negativity, harsh feelings, and unnecessary work that is endured in schools and districts alike can be tied back to poor communication. This reality begs the question, *is poor communication the root of all evil?*

I remember standing in a room full of people and trying to navigate the emotional sentiments of a group of parents that I could attribute back to a lack of effective communication on my part. I had known the kind of fallout that would come from my decision, and maybe that is what led to my failure to communicate information in a timely manner. Essentially, I was putting off the inevitable. Yes, I could have told them honestly that the previous week had been hectic and that I had been trying to navigate what seemed like a bazillion things that were coming my way. Quite frankly, people don't want to hear excuses, especially from a leader who prides himself on owning his mistakes. So I did the only thing I could do in that moment: I apologized.

Later that evening as I reflected on my failure to properly communicate with some of my stakeholders, I began to think about the types of issues educators deal with that stem from poor communication. In truth, poor communication—and the trouble it causes—is not isolated to schools, but can be seen in almost all organizations, including public and private businesses. If we acknowledge the value of good communication and are proactive with our efforts (even when we know we may not get a positive response), it is possible to avoid the kind of awkward moment I endured that evening in front of my stakeholders. Here are a few commonly problematic situations, as well as suggestions, for improving communication with your students and staff members:

1. **Timely communication is vital.** If "last minute" becomes the norm, people will begin to question your effectiveness as a leader. Great leaders recognize this and lean on a team of other teachers and support staff to help keep them organized and hold them accountable.

2. **If there is a concern or issue that needs to be addressed, it is best to have the conversation in person rather than via email.** If you are the one who receives a contentious online communication, respond by asking if you can meet face-to-face to discuss the concern.

3. **If you are concerned about the way something was communicated or don't agree with a decision that was made, go to the source of the information/communication and clarify or question the decision.** Gossiping to others about a decision or the way it was communicated will not resolve your issue, but learning more about the situation/decision may help you better understand the supporting reasons and underlying circumstances.

4. **There is no excuse for not contacting a parent whose student is failing a class.** Failing to do so makes you party to the failure. The conversation is sure to take on a more emotional and negative tone if the communication comes after the final grade has been given.

5. **If you know of a student that is struggling who has typically been successful in school, take time to seek out that student and ask what you can do to help them be successful and then follow up with a phone call to a parent.** The mere fact that you took time to ask and call will help build trust with your students and parents.

6. **Avoid sarcasm and defensiveness.** Never ask a student to repeat an inappropriate comment you clearly heard the first time because you are upset and want to use it as ammunition to punish the offender. Don't make it about you.

7. **If you are having difficulty contacting a parent or you are unable to reach a parent altogether due to a non-working number, seek the assistance of an administrator immediately and ask them to help you make contact.** This is one way they will see you being proactive in trying to help students be successful.

8. **If you are dealing with student behavior issues, stay out in front of it by communicating early on.** The last thing you want is to wait for things to build to a boiling point and then inundate a parent at your first meeting with a laundry list of miscues by the student.

9. **If you are a director or coach who has decided that a student who has previously taken a starring or starting role in events or games will not perform or play (or take**

a lead or starting position), take time to sit down face-
to-face and explain to the student why the decision was
made and what it means for his or her role moving forward. Follow this up with a phone call (not email or text) to
a parent so they can remain informed.

10. **If you are a witness to a good deed, be sure to make it a
priority to validate that person's good work in person or
through a personal note.** If it involves a student, a positive
phone call home can be a game changer for many kids and
parents who are not conditioned to hearing positive comments coming from schools.

I don't think we can ever go wrong with over-communicating
if we are doing it effectively. We must recognize that the timeliness
and quality of our communication can affect our connection to each
individual member of our community and have an impact on each
person's success as well as the success and culture of the entire organization. Over the years I have learned that the way we condition our
students, staff, and parents to respond to our communication ultimately will determine our success as an organization. Maximizing
our effectiveness and our success, then, requires us to make communication personal, direct, clear, and kind so that poor communication
does not take root and succumb to evil.

Leaders Own Their Morale

For years, school leaders have reported that faculty and staff tell
them they are unhappy in the workplace. And for years, administrators have responded to those concerns in various ways with limited
success. Many have tried to get a "true" measure of this perception
and its causes by conducting building or district-wide culture surveys. The hope is that by collecting feedback, schools will be able to

determine the contributing factors to morale issues so that appropriate action plans can be put into place to address any concerns. Districts may even use a third-party vendor to conduct the survey in hope of getting honest feedback. Eventually, the results of those surveys are shared with all employees and everyone sees the baseline measurement of employee satisfaction and engagement level. Sometimes the results can be deeply concerning, indicating staff members are feeling disengaged, uninspired, and dissatisfied.

But what happens when the results indicate the exact opposite—that staff is feeling engaged, inspired, and very satisfied? Should you just check "create positive culture" off your to-do list and move on? Maybe not. In some cases, although it may appear as if all is well in the Land of Oz, the reality is that your staff members are dissatisfied with the survey and feel the questions didn't allow them a "true" opportunity to have their voices heard. After all, a bubble sheet doesn't always work with student assessment. Why should we expect such simple metrics to work when what people really want is an opportunity to air their concerns in writing and/or verbally?

When it comes to culturizing a school or district, the first step is ensuring staff members look forward to coming to work each day. People should beam with pride when asked about their job, school, and school district. If they love coming to work and morale is positive, they will be in a better place emotionally and mentally to give their best to kids. A positive work environment is the most critical element of ensuring that students feel safe, connected, valued, and primed for success. In addition, when morale is high, staff not only look forward to coming to work each day, they also look forward to going home each night and can further give their best to their families, and that is just as important.

No teacher or leader likes to be criticized or feel unappreciated, especially if they feel they devote everything to being and giving their

> **A positive work environment is the most critical element of ensuring that students feel safe, connected, valued, and primed for success.**

best. However, as teachers and leaders, we must own up to our part in morale issues as well as our responsibility for improving student and staff morale.

One way as a school leader that you can "own" this morale is to meet with members of your school/district leadership team one-on-one and ask them to be candid with you about what they and their colleagues believe to be the areas that are impacting staff morale. Of course, in doing so, you will need to ask them for their trust—the kind of trust that believes you won't violate their trust in you by getting defensive or hurt by their comments, even if the comment is about your (lack of) effectiveness as a leader. If you want them to be honest, they'll need to trust that you will respond positively and act to improve the areas they think need attention.

Although these conversations may lead to some moments of initial discomfort, they need to happen if positive change of any magnitude is going to occur. Honest discussions open the door for the school to develop a high-performing team that understands that the role of culturizing a school environment is everyone's responsibility. As leaders, we must be willing to describe and communicate in a positive way our own feelings about morale while modeling vulnerability, honesty, and personal responsibility. Here are five ways to help you address classroom, building, and/or district morale issues:

1. **Communication.** Communication is one thing; effective communication is another. Most teachers and leaders will tell you they believe they communicate, but as I noted in the previous section, not all communication is *effective* communication. In addition to knowing what's going on in the organization, people need to know what you stand for. Let your students, colleagues, and staff members know what you are passionate about, what you believe in, what you think, and what you believe needs to happen next. Our best people and our students want to do a great job, but they also need to know what we expect from them.

2. **Trust.** Asking for your team's trust is only the first step. Building real trust takes time. It's done when you maintain your team members' confidence—by not taking things personally, by not becoming defensive, and by trying not to offer an explanation (or excuse) every time you hear something you don't like. Listen and accept the feedback you asked for when you asked to be trusted. When they are taking the risk to be honest with you, it is the time to listen, not talk.

3. **Placing blame.** We must always take responsibility for our results. It is too easy to pass the buck or make excuses for why we didn't achieve the results we wanted. By placing blame, we only give others a reason to question our integrity and our leadership (in whatever position we hold). It's especially important to avoid placing blame on others if you are a school or district leader. Remember, you don't want your team members worrying about how you will respond when their own performance or actions are the ones being questioned. This is the time to use "I" or "We" statements in your explanations and/or your responses.

4. **Team builder.** One of the core principles of building a successful organization is developing a team atmosphere. Leaders should not delegate team building responsibility to others. No matter how many team-building activities you do or how many facilitators you bring in to help your organization's members gel as a team, the results won't be there unless you model what it means to be part of a team. How you interact, respond to, and acknowledge the work of others daily demonstrates your awareness that you can't do this alone. If you want to improve the team mentality in your school or district, be intentional about establishing meaningful and purposeful relationships with each member of the team.

5. **Follow through.** When someone shares a concern or asks for feedback or whenever you take time to address an individual or building-wide issue that has been brought to your attention, be sure to follow up, communicate a plan, and then act. People don't expect their school leaders to resolve every issue, but they do expect them to listen, gather information,

> **No matter how many team-building activities you do or how many facilitators you bring in to help your organization's members gel as a team, the results won't be there unless you model what it means to be part of a team.**

seek out the cause of the issue, communicate what we find, and then take some action to try to resolve it. Demonstrate that you value your team members' opinions and feedback and are willing to follow through with action.

If not addressed appropriately, poor morale will threaten a team's ability to work effectively. But when both teachers and leaders (whether they have a leadership title or not) take ownership of their part in improving morale, the organization has the chance to shift from average to excellence. By building communities, building others up, and building in a sense of trust, we can create the kind of positive work environment where adults want to work and students want to learn.

Expect Excellence

All successful schools share one key thing in common: a core group of leaders (teachers and administrators) who believe 1) they can change the world, and 2) the success of their students and staff starts with the expectation of excellence. They expect the best from others and even more from themselves. They focus on their own personal and professional growth, and they set a standard for others to do the same. They understand that expecting excellence from themselves is a choice, but striving for excellence each day is a lifestyle and the first step in modeling what they expect from others.

Striving for excellence each day is a lifestyle.

CULTURE BUILDER #1

Team Resolve—The best way to begin to address any cultural issue is through conversation, investment, communication, and action. Try modeling this process with your school leadership team (or classroom). Create an environment that allows every voice to be heard and where everyone plays a role in culturizing the school. Begin by sitting down and talking to each person privately. Don't be afraid to ask for candid feedback and compile responses in general themes. As each person describes areas that need improving, you will then need to inject the most critical component to this process. That component is asking each member the following question: "What are you willing to invest to help me address this concern?" The message being sent with this question is that you need their help in making this change happen and that you cannot do this alone. Share the feedback you collect with the entire group and ask them to review the information with their teams (which could be based on grade level, floor, department team, etc.) and bring comments back to the entire group. Next, work together to prioritize the responses and allow people (or teams) to select the areas they want to address first, once again asking for their personal investment in helping resolve the issue. After you've come to an agreement on what needs your personal attention, communicate to the entire staff (or classroom) the recommendations that were decided based on their input that need considerable attention, and communicate your plan for improving your practices.

Throughout the year, be sure to continue to communicate your goal areas and touch base with others to confirm progress with the areas they are addressing. At the end of the year, meet one-on-one with each school leadership team member to revisit your conversation from the year prior, and ask them to comment on your goal areas as well as include new issues that need attention. You will find that the vulnerability you initially felt when soliciting feedback face-to-face is replaced with a sense of relief because you have grown personally, your staff members feel heard and respected, *and* your team now knows they are not solely dependent on you to address every morale issue.

CULTURE BUILDER #2

Boost Your Sanctuary—Take inventory and determine whether your school offices breed culture builders or culture killers. Remember that every person in your organization helps to establish its culture. Offices that have been culturized were created by design, not by default or serendipity. Take time to examine your office areas with a critical eye. Ask a trusted colleague from another school to give you honest feedback on how they were treated as they entered the main office. Here are a few ways for you to quickly gauge your main office climate:

- Take notice of the faces of those who both work and visit your main office. Do their faces shine bright or do they appear stressed and burdened?

- Listen to the words being spoken, but more importantly *how* they are being spoken. Is the tone kind and sincere or harsh and tempered?

- Are conversations positive and focused on how they can help others, or are they self-serving and negative?

- Are telephone calls and guests greeted in a manner that leaves the other person feeling welcomed and valued?

- Are all students welcomed with a sincere and friendly "Hello, it is so good to see you!"? Even those who may be there for disciplinary reasons?

- Are the walls, desks, and counters adorned with authentic items that celebrate student success?

- Does the look of the environment present itself in a professional way that represents great pride and a tradition of excellence? The main office gives the first impression of how well the rest of the building is maintained.

- When you finish rating the climate of your main office, follow up with the rest of your offices throughout the building.

School offices must serve as sanctuaries where people can come to have their spirits boosted, not suppressed. As a space that sees hundreds of interactions per day, the school office atmosphere can either diminish or enhance the experiences of members of our school communities. Be the leader who sets the tone of the guiding principles that serve as a model of how you want others to be treated.

CULTURE BUILDER #3

Beyond the Check Box—We should strive to create a culture where people have a burning desire to succeed as opposed to just checking items off their lists. Examine what you are currently asking others in your organization to do that results in them simply checking the box without any thought, effort, or investment in the activity. Even when to-do lists are implemented with good intentions, over time they can become mindless tasks that lose their meaning and value.

- **Handbook Regulations and Classroom Rules.** Re-examine when the best time to review these items should be. Staff welcome back? No. First day of class? No. I strongly recommend pushing them back and spreading them out over a period of weeks. Use the first few days and weeks of school to invest in personal relationships.

- **In-service Trainings.** Nothing is less fun than discussing blood-borne pathogens, mandatory reporting, and bullying training. Are these things important? Yes! Are these things necessary to review at the beginning of the new school year? I don't think so. Consider having your staff complete this training at home or online during the summer before returning to school. Give this time back to teachers to spend in their classrooms.

- **Summer Retreats.** Your team will not invest in this process unless you come prepared with a specific agenda and focus. All retreats should be held off-campus. Otherwise, don't call it a retreat; call it just another all-day meeting. Effective retreats focus on team bonding, genuinely investing in each other, sharing with and learning from one another, and dreaming and planning for ways to make the upcoming school year the best ever.

- **Professional Development.** PD loses impact if teachers see it as a checkbox activity. Add meaning back into PD by differentiating (just as we expect teachers to do for students to demonstrate learning). Perhaps a reflection form followed by discussion, conversation with members of your building leadership team or administration about takeaways or next steps, or a more formal presentation to show how they benefitted and what it could mean for them, their team, or their students.

- **Surveys.** This has become one of the biggest check boxes in schools today. Why? Because we are either not reviewing the responses with fidelity, are struggling where to begin and therefore don't do anything with the results, or are not effectively communicating what we are doing with them. If you cannot get a handle on these responses, you will continue to lose credibility as a teacher/principal/superintendent. As a team, review the results of any survey given, discuss as a team, determine next steps, set goals, assign a timeline, communicate progress, and celebrate your successes, no matter how small they may be. Then revisit again and again.

- **District Strategic Plan/School Improvement Plans.** Generally speaking, strategic plans are not reviewed often enough to guide our vision and work on a daily basis. When we don't use these plans to make decisions in a strategic and systemic way, teachers and leaders quickly figure out that the document doesn't really serve a purpose, and they quit investing in the process that was used to gather the information and develop the plan.

- **Hiring Process.** Nothing is more important than selecting the right people for your team. Yet administrators often complain about the hiring season and the amount of time this process takes. I get it. It does take a lot of time, but hiring for excellence should never be taken lightly. So check yourself, and make sure your attitude is in the right place from the first interview until the last hire.

Our students and teachers deserve for us to respect their time by assigning only meaningful tasks and asking them to participate in activities that really matter. When we approach necessary items such as the ones listed above in a more purposeful way, we demonstrate that we honor their work and time.

Educators in successful schools understand that their primary responsibility is to build a community where everyone has the opportunity to demonstrate their own capacity to lead and genuinely see themselves as leaders. Leadership gets put into action by focusing on the simple things: engaging everyone in conversation, supervising and acknowledging students in a positive manner, showing up on time, taking notes and being "present" during staff meetings, or calling parents simply because they wanted to acknowledge their child's effort in class or to say thank you for their support.

Those who expect the best from others accept the fact that sometimes they will have to say no to a student or colleague, even though they know that saying yes would be the easier path to take. At the same time, they never play "gotcha" games, because they are motivated more by celebrating small successes than they are trying to catch students and staff doing wrong. They also don't accept the status quo and aren't afraid to push back, especially when they see others not giving their best effort or when their negativity begins to impact the climate of a meeting or the classroom. They model this through their communication. They value and respect the time, place, and manner in which they communicate because they know that ineffective communication often results in an issue being unnecessarily created. Educators who have remained positive over the years have figured out they are happier when they own their own morale rather than depend on others or place blame somewhere else for their attitude. Those who expect excellence believe they don't need a title in front of their name to be a leader.

Are you ready to lead that charge? If so, it will require you to lead by example. No longer will you be able to expect your students or colleagues to do what you are not willing to do yourself. To be a strong and effective leader, you will need to have the same expectations of others that you have of yourself. Moreover, you will need to model it in a way that when others think of excellence, they think of you.

QUESTIONS FOR DISCUSSION

» What characteristics could you point out in others to help them understand what it means to expect excellence?

» How has your response to a situation where you didn't know what to do helped you become a better teacher or administrator?

» What qualities does an untitled leader possess that allow him or her to influence others to strive for excellence?

» Share specific examples of what the people in your organization do to help one another live their excellence. What else can you do to support your team?

CHAPTER 4
CORE PRINCIPLE 3:
Carry the Banner

Your culture of your organization will
be defined by the worst behavior you
are willing to tolerate.

—Todd Whitaker, Steve Gruenert,
School Culture Rewired

Afew years ago, I had the good fortune of visiting with a former teacher from my district. The teacher, Ben, informed me that he had been offered an assistant principal position at the middle school where he currently worked. I was happy for him, and as he shared his story about his interview for the position, I knew the hiring board had made the right decision. Ben's energy, passion, and excitement were evident as he spoke about his students and his school. But I'm willing to bet that the following comment Ben made is what sealed the offer: "I told the superintendent that I was ready to be an assistant principal, that I wanted to be a leader at that school and not anywhere else." He *loved* his work. Ben talked so positively about the school, the students, and the current staff. "We are young," he said, "but the staff that is there really believes in the kids and wants to be there."

When you work in a school that has a reputation for being "challenging," it is easy to fall into the trap of talking negatively about the school, the community, the staff, the students—or any other available, contributing factor. The last administrative team with whom I worked referred to this verbal bashing as *awfulizing*. You'll recognize *awfulizers* by their habit of complaining about students, colleagues, parents, lack of resources, the administration, mandates, and any other decision with which they disagree. What is lost in those who awfulize is that others are listening to them and then transferring that message to others in the school community. Over time, the negative comments have a cumulative, damaging effect, and the school gets labeled (often unfairly so) as a poor-performing school with low morale, a negative environment, or worse yet, as a school that doesn't care about its students.

In contrast, teachers, staff members, and administrators who abide by the third core principle carry the banner for their schools and harbor a deep adulation, sense of honor, and great regard for the schools and districts in which they serve—and it shows in their words and actions. They understand that their work isn't about them; it's about their students and their families, their colleagues, and the communities in which they serve. They speak passionately and positively about their school community, illuminating it in every conversation at every opportunity. Ben's words reflected the heart of someone who understood the importance of being an ambassador for his organization. He provided an example for what it meant to lift up a school with a message of honor, commitment, and solidarity.

Here are three ways in which your vibe as an educator can attract a tribe of people who are willing to carry the banner for your school or district:

- **Model positive interactions.** Effective educators never stop modeling positive interactions. They recognize that every interaction with a student, parent, or staff member is one single moment to inspire more positive interactions and to impact every person they encounter in a positive way. Our organizations and, quite frankly, our profession would be so much better off if we just modeled this one simple act at every opportunity. Be that moment for others.

- **Remember that your body language reflects your beliefs.** One practical way you can ensure you bring your best *you* into every situation is to bring a positive attitude—regardless of the severity of the situation. Never forget that your body is listening to everything your mind says. If your mindset is projecting an attitude of "we shall overcome," then your body language and actions will mirror your beliefs. You become what you believe.

- **Show appreciation.** A person who feels valued and appreciated will always do and give more than what is expected. Educators who have been blessed to be surrounded by a caring and thoughtful team understand the significance of a simple thank you, pat on the back, handwritten note, or an occasional gift that comes with a personal touch of a shared prior experience. The most heartfelt message we can share with others is our genuine gratitude.

The job of a teacher and school administrator is taxing. As I stated earlier in the book, what other profession do you know that requires its members to do a year's worth of work in nine months and do it with all the emotion, patience, and investment of a surrogate parent? How many times have you pulled into your driveway and walked into your home exhausted and emotionally spent with nothing left to give your own family? Or walked down the hallway and out the doors feeling empty inside because you couldn't get through to a student like you wanted to and then questioned your ability to make an impact? I am guessing it happens regularly for many of you. Yet, you know tomorrow is another day, so like many of your colleagues, you dig down deep, keep the faith, and continue to carry the banner for your students and for each other. You keep giving everything you have every day to serve others in order to rekindle that spirit and refuel your own and others' energy through genuine conversations that provide a dose of inspiration for a better tomorrow.

Great Change Begins with Self-Change

Being an educator can be an isolating profession. To experience what it feels like to have the responsibility of educating other people's children every day, every evening, every weekend, can be overwhelming. Working in schools can take its toll, especially when we allow doubt to creep in, which causes us to question whether we can truly make a difference. But if we understand that even the simplest of comments or words of encouragement can make a life-changing impact on our students, the job seems a little less daunting. When we take time to invest in conversations with others, we are often pleasantly surprised by the smiles these interactions bring to our faces and the warmth they can bring to our hearts. I still remember Mr. Morgan and how he interacted with me and my parents. It made a difference in more ways than he might have ever imagined. Even more so, he would tell others that I was a good kid with lots of potential. That's how we carry the banner for students and for each other: one conversation and one interaction at a time. Little by little we connect, support, and encourage, and by doing so, we begin to create a positive culture for our students and our school communities. And we don't speak negatively about those we serve or support. We can have the best of intentions and tell our students and our colleagues that we care about them, that they are important to us, that we are here to support them to be successful, and that we will not let them fail; however, carrying the banner for our students and our colleagues means we will maintain such support even when they fail to live up to our expectations. Each of us possesses the power to be a difference maker for every student, every day. We must also be willing to do whatever it takes and not give up on our parents, teachers, and administrators. Our schools don't need more *awfulizers*; they need more *awesomizers*!

You can be that awesomizer! It won't be a one-size-fits all program, textbook, or teaching method that makes a difference for your students. It will be you. It will be the way you pause and make one child at a time feel valued rather than invisible. It will be the encouragement you offer to a struggling student or the chance you take to show a little faith and be an advocate for a student whom others just "don't get." Every student and every staff member deserve to work in an environment where they are given the opportunity to leave their legacy because someone is carrying a banner for them.

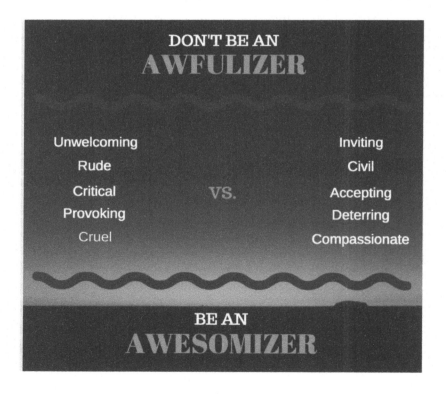

What We Model Is What We Get

Educators who carry the banner work a tremendous number of hours and do their best to make a positive impact in their school communities. The experience our students and colleagues have in schools today depends greatly on how we behave and the way we communicate to members of our school community. It is often not what we say, but rather how we say it. In some cases, it's what we don't say that creates a culture of mistrust or, worse, leads to a negative school/work experience for those whom we are entrusted to teach and serve. We must continue to give back to our profession and support our colleagues and potential future colleagues in their endeavors. Learning is critical, but learning from each other is even more critical if we do not want the success of our school communities left to chance.

I have had the opportunity to observe hundreds of teachers in my career. By watching others, I've learned that the best teachers....

- Model a love for learning

- Value personal and trusting relationships

- Are extremely passionate

- Are empathetic

- Model risk-taking and encourage their students to do the same

- Are flexible and make adjustments based on student feedback

- Recognize learning goes both ways

- Focus on what kids are doing, not what they aren't doing

- Teach kids, not content

- Have students tell them where they are so they know from where to build

- Strive to be their best for their students

- See students as partners

- Prepare assignments as if they were for themselves

- Aim to figure out what is going on with each student so as to better understand them and their thinking.

- Push students and their thinking and encourage them to strive for greatness

- Understand that the kids who frustrate them the most are the kids who need them the most

- Try to catch students doing things right

- Try not to bottle kids up

- Want students to have a better school experience than their own and to experience success

- Want to find a connection with kids by showing them they care, not just telling them

- Feed off student energy and then give it back

- Stay active in the classroom

- Try to learn something from a student every day

- Share a small bit of kindness every day

- Take time to acknowledge each student and recognize their work and progress

- Create unique experiences

- Accept that teaching is a calling—a mission

- Have an appreciation for the hard work of co-teachers and leaders

- Apologize to students and parents when they are wrong
- Honor the individual talents and struggles students bring to the class and try to inspire them to move forward
- Understand and are sensitive to the fact that kids have different needs
- Try to instill a sense of confidence in all students
- Accept they are responsible for the successes and failures of their students
- Believe all kids are good

Whether we are beginning a new school year, returning from holiday break or an extended weekend, or kicking off a new week on Monday morning, the onus is on us to model the attitudes and behaviors we want to see repeated. Our spoken words and the positive way we conduct ourselves can be the catalysts that can spark change and culturize a school community that yields success for all students, both through their eyes as well as through the eyes of each member of the school community.

Our spoken words and the positive way we conduct ourselves can be the catalysts that can spark change and culturize a school community that yields success for all students.

Eyes on Culture by Sarah Peakin

Principal's Secretary, Bettendorf High School, Bettendorf, Iowa

I have always respected and admired individuals who work in education. I have many connections in education: a grandfather who was on a school board, a mother who was a para educator, a husband who was a teacher and is now an administrator, and numerous other friends and family members who work in education. I, however, knew I didn't have the skill set for teaching, so I took to the business route and worked in various human resource roles.

When my husband and I relocated with two small children, I learned about a position as a principal's secretary. I knew I could perform the job duties necessary, but I was hesitant about one thing: working closely with high school students. Nine years later, I would tell you that it's my favorite part of my job! There are so many examples of students who have taught me, made an impact on my life, or shown me the true meaning of perseverance.

One student often comes to mind. She was frequently sent to the principal's office due to constant attendance issues, classroom disruptions, and the occasional fight. She could be defiant with faculty and strong willed and stubborn with other students. As a secretary, I don't issue any discipline, but I am often the first person with whom students interact when they are in trouble. Through multiple conversations, often while the student served a detention in our office, I learned about her complicated story. Despite the challenges she faced, over time she began to focus on her education and steer clear of drama—and she got on the path toward graduation.

I never would have guessed I had an impact on her life, but on one of her last days of school, she left me a note that said, "I appreciate everything you've done for me from large to small. I'll always keep your kind words and smile with me." I realized then that it's not always the big things you do for students that make a difference. The daily positive interactions you have with students can have a profound impact. I keep this handwritten note taped to my desk along with my children's artwork because it reminds me of the importance of a smile and small gestures.

Working in a busy main office of a high school is not quiet, and I rarely get my to-do list done, but I have learned that isn't the most important part of my job. My most important job is to be available to students whether they need someone to talk to, a safe place to calm down, or maybe they just need a mint and a smile.

I respect administrators and teachers, knowing I couldn't do their jobs, so I attempt to assist them any way I can. Throughout all the challenges, frustrations, laughter, and tears, it is all worth it when students walk across that stage at graduation prepared to take on their next challenge.

Positive Energy Equals Synergy

There isn't a day that goes by in the work of an educator that is free of challenges. The never-ending stream of problems that flows across our paths during the course of a school year can leave even the most positive and passionate teachers and leaders exhausted and depleted. It is easy to get sucked into the minutia of the daily grind and fall into the trap of dealing with trivial things that drain our energy and overfill our plates.

What can you do to provide yourself with a little bit of reprieve and stay fresh and energized? Scrape a few things off your plate and shift your focus. Consider a new perspective on how others see you and on how your attitude impacts your students, staff members, and community. Are you offering energy and hope to others? When you realize how your attitude and actions set an example and affects others, you might just decide to change the way you think, dream, plan, and act. Reflect on the following thoughts to help keep things in perspective:

- **Reflect vs. Deflect.** At the heart of every problem is a conversation to be had. As educators, you cannot fall into the trap of deflecting conversations about concerns or issues that are brought to your attention. I believe problems can be resolved when each person is willing to listen and reflect on what is really being said by the other. It's when we take time to pause and reflect that we truly grow as problem solvers.

> It's when we take time to pause and reflect that we truly grow as problem solvers.

- **Reinvest vs. Invest.** Take time to reinvest in your veteran staff members. It's easy to get so caught up in the excitement of investing in new teachers that the professional development needs of veteran teachers get forgotten. If you are a school leader, be intentional about tapping into the years of valuable experience, knowledge, and wisdom that can be passed on from one generation of teachers to the next. At the same time, be intentional about providing meaningful, ongoing, professional development opportunities for your seasoned teachers. If you are a teacher, make the commitment to never stop investing in your own learning and sharing your learning with others at every level within your organization.

- **Aspire vs. Inspire.** You can't inspire your students and colleagues to be great if you are not aspiring for greatness yourself. You must aspire so you can inspire! That doesn't mean you won't ever fall short of your goals; it means you're willing to be courageous and vulnerable in order to make the impact. You set the example. Model the kind of attitudes and behaviors you hope to inspire in others.

- **Act vs. React.** The surest way to lose your students' and colleagues' confidence is by failing to act. Fear of making the wrong decision often keeps people from making *any* decision. The irony is that by *not* deciding, you *are* making a decision: the decision to not act! That indecision and inaction then thrusts you into reaction mode, which can create a feeling of frustration on the part of your students and colleagues. If indecision and inaction become your pattern, it will damage your credibility as an effective teacher or leader. There is nothing wrong with doing your due diligence in gathering information before making a decision (I recommend it), but then take action on what you learn so you aren't forced into a position where you have to react.

Overall, educators feel a tremendous moral obligation to work until the work is done, whether we are grading papers, responding to emails, or contacting parents. We worry about what others will think about the quality of our work or whether we are the right person for the job. We make assumptions that others are speaking poorly about us, and those negative thoughts mess with our heads. But to eliminate negative energy and increase positive energy and synergy in our schools, we must be intentional about our mindsets and attitudes. That means we must stop worrying about others' attitudes and expectations and focus on our own mindsets and behaviors and how they affect others. In doing so, we have the power to improve how we feel, which has an impact on the way we act—and on how those around us act.

Focus on Life-Fit, Not Balance

I first heard the term *life-fit* a few years back during a conversation with the director of professional learning for school administrators of Iowa. She used the phrase in reference to the way educators manage their time between their professional responsibilities and their personal obligations. I love the way she described life-fit: "It's looking at how we, as teachers and school leaders, reduce stress by creating an ebb and flow that works for us. Often the word *balance* carries a negative connotation in that it suggests the goal is to find a fifty-fifty split between work and life, and if we are not meeting that goal, we must be doing something wrong.".

I was so intrigued by what she shared with me that I asked if she could send me any information she had on the topic of balance vs. life-fit. Here's what I've learned:

Balance	**VS.**	**Life-Fit**

Balance	**Life-Fit**
1. Is most frequently discussed in the negative	1. Honors our unique situations throughout various points in our lives
2. Keeps us focused on the problem rather than the solution	2. Leads us to inspire
3. Assumes we are all the same	3. Recognizes multiple options based upon each person's current circumstances
4. Infers there is a "right" answer	4. Acknowledges the ebb and flow of life's events
5. Leads us to judge	5. Values flexibility
6. Results in unproductive guilt	
7. Leaves no room for periods where there is more work and less life and vice versa	
8. Ignores the constantly changing reality of work and life	

As you think about your perspective and mindset regarding work, considering life-fit may help you reduce any struggle you may feel to balance your passion for education with your commitment to family and personal well-being. I have seen so many caring, effective teachers and leaders be consumed by guilt because they were not able to meet a deadline, attend a school activity, give more personal attention to a struggling student/teacher/family, or help a colleague supervise a school event. You may feel that same guilt rise up in your own life when it seems that, regardless of the hours you put in, you can't seem to meet the needs of your school community. There's an ever-present sense that you should have done something more.

We must recognize and accept that there will always be more work to do, more deadlines to meet, another situation to resolve, and that our email inbox, if it ever does reach zero, will only remain at zero for a few minutes. Life-fit addresses not *what we feel we should do* but *what we can actually do* and acknowledges that those aren't always the same.

Striving for life-fit gives us permission to do what works for us—without judgment or guilt. Life-fit is different for everyone. Life-fit looks different for a first-year administrator who is single from that of someone who is married and has three small children. Life-fit looks different for a teacher whose children are grown and now has more time to devote to other people's children. Life-fit looks different for a staff member whose spouse also works full time and whose work requires a lot of travel as opposed to someone whose spouse is a stay-at-home parent. Life-fit honors our unique situations throughout various points in our lives. Finding a life-fit allows us to be forgiving of ourselves and to recognize there are ebbs and flows to life's events.

> **Finding a life-fit allows us to be forgiving of ourselves and to recognize there are ebbs and flows to life's events.**

Starting today, what are some things you can do to support life-fit so you can be at your best and serve others well?

1. Be purposeful in scheduling down time.
2. Drop activities that zap your time and energy.
3. Set aside time weekly to do something you truly enjoy doing and honor it.
4. Consider what can you delegate to someone else.
5. Trust that others will follow through on your expectations.
6. Take care of your body by exercising and making healthy food choices.

As educators, our work is never finished. It is how we manage our time and energy that determines our effectiveness in carrying the banner for others. Taking the perspective of life-fit over life-balance empowers us to support and allows for flexibility for ourselves and those around us, which in turn allows us to create a culture that energizes (rather than drains) the very people we aim to serve.

Becoming #FutureReady

Three years ago I was sitting in a room with over one hundred of our country's most innovative school superintendents. We'd been invited by the White House to commit to a pledge of cultivating a culture of digital learning in their school districts. This was to be accomplished by working with students, educators, families, and members of the community to become future ready. It was truly one of the most incredible, life-changing opportunities that ever came my way.

I remember being completely moved from the speeches by Deputy Assistant to the President for Education Roberto Rodriguez, U.S. Secretary of Education Arne Duncan, and the President of the United States, Barack Obama. As I sat and listened to each of them speak, I felt inspired to act. But the questions that kept running through my head were the same questions every educator faces daily:

- What action can I take that will make the greatest impact on my school community as well as students and families across the state and country?

- How can I move forward with a sense of urgency so that the passion, hope, and energy they feel doesn't fade away when faced with challenges?

On the flight home, I reviewed my notes from the event, and a comment shared by Secretary Duncan struck a chord with me: "We must close the opportunity gap first before we can begin the work of closing the achievement gap for kids." It was a call to action for us to commit to identifying and providing opportunities for all members of our school communities as well as with those members of our personal and professional networks. The work is too great for the load to fall solely on the shoulders of superintendents to bring about Future Ready opportunities that will lead to Future Ready change. Our focus needs to shift to providing opportunities for leaders, teachers, and students to come together on a regular basis to help carry the load. If we truly believe that every individual has the capacity to lead, then perhaps the success of our organizations should be measured by the number of opportunities we provide for others to demonstrate their leadership and impact on both the personal and professional learning by all members of our school communities. I would suggest that Future Ready change requires the following:

1. **Opportunities for leaders to come together.** Taking on a leadership role at any level is tough. It takes courage, resiliency, and the tenacity to withstand the barrage of challenges, negativity, and stress that comes with most leadership roles.

And yet here we sit trying to navigate this journey alone, our thoughts, ideas, and worries isolated from our peers and sometimes our own families. Future Ready change will require us to surround ourselves with a network of excellence to nurture our own need for personal and professional growth. We must act by cultivating opportunities for teams of leaders to come together in more meaningful ways. One recommendation would be for superintendents to make the time to come together in one another's school districts during PD/meeting days and learn from one another by observing model programs, sharing resources, and discussing best practices. By doing so, they could take advantage of every opportunity to come together as a consortium of leaders and create a learning opportunity for themselves and for their school districts. This could be done by regularly visiting their neighbors in school districts across the state rather than meeting in sterile, isolated locations.

2. **Opportunities for teachers to grow and develop their craft.** Being a lifelong learner is no easy task. It takes time, effort, commitment, focus, discipline, desire, and a sense of vulnerability to push ourselves to the next level. Yet with the right support and level of trust, most educators would not only aspire to reach the next level but would want to achieve a greater sense of accomplishment for themselves to have a greater impact on their students. Future Ready change will require us to provide meaningful teacher-led professional development by both new and veteran teachers to create a culture where all teachers feel valued for their expertise and contribution to a school's success. We must find ways to highlight teacher and student projects, learning in our schools, and using social and local media to showcase the

very best. We will also need to invest, re-invest, and trust in our teachers by providing opportunities for them to attend state and national conferences as a team. In these, they'll support a collaborative culture that will move the barometer needle from pockets of excellence to a network of excellence to a system of excellence that ensures equity for all.

3. **Opportunities for students to showcase their character, talents, and brilliance.** Creating a platform to spotlight student voice requires trust, belief, high expectations, patience, intentional fortitude, and a mindset that students can provide meaningful content, conversation, and feedback and can represent our schools in a positive manner. As far as we have come in providing students a stage to demonstrate their learning in authentic, non-traditional, and meaningful ways, we have landed short of flattening the hierarchy that exists in schools today when it comes to placing a value on the student voice and developing student agency. This opportunity gap is even more noticeable at the elementary and middle school levels. Future Ready change is going to require us to be more consistent and thorough in providing student-led initiatives that give students a voice in curriculum offerings, school policies, design of classroom and other learning spaces, lesson/unit design, student-led conferences, and feedback on teacher effectiveness in the classroom. In addition, we will need to see more shifts in classroom instruction with consistent implementation of practices such as genius hour, 20% time, gamification activities, project-based learning, student presentations, personalized learning models, and other student led learning options that require students to demonstrate their learning through presentation, modeling, and performance.

We cannot continue to sequester our leaders, teachers, and students if we want to inspire our communities to be Future Ready. We must continually think beyond ourselves and not look at this challenge as an individual, school, or district competition. We must see it as an opportunity to come together as a collaborative community and carry the banner to be the Future Ready change for a nation of schools our children and parents relish.

A Moment to Remember

I was sixteen years old when I watched Lorenzo Charles grab Dereck Whittenberg's desperation air ball and slam home the winner at the buzzer in the 1983 NCAA Basketball Championship Final. I will never forget the joy I felt watching Coach Jim Valvano running madly around the court in utter jubilation looking for someone to hug.

For fifteen years, I was fortunate to serve as a camp coach for Iowa Hawkeye Basketball. I traveled the Midwest giving dribbling clinics and serving as a camp coach to many young players. One of my favorite memories was serving as a referee during the league games. I often used my "magic whistle" to impact the final seconds of the basketball games, and my goal was always the same: end with a tie. My reason was simple. You see, camp rules stated that if the game ended in a tie, then the game would be decided by pressure free throws, with the player standing at the free throw line surrounded by players yelling and screaming and trying to distract the shooter. This meant that some young player would have the opportunity to have a camp moment they would never forget: a tie-game, no-time-left-on-the-clock, pressure free throw for the win. One free throw away from their shining moment: a moment they would remember for their rest of their lives, win or lose!

Those exhilarating moments can be hard to come by, but I remember one that I had the opportunity to witness during my early years as a principal. It's a moment that made an impression on me and its memory still makes me smile, and I know it's a moment one young man will never forget. It was near the end of the basketball season and our boys' team was playing our cross-town rival for bragging rights and first place in the conference. The noise level in the jam-packed gym was deafening. It was nearing half time, and although we were ahead, the momentum had clearly shifted and the other team was making a run and threatening to head to the locker room with the lead. With less than a minute left in the half, our post player picked up his second foul of the game.

Earlier in the week, my basketball coach, Kevin Skillett (@krskillett), told me he was having a difficult time keeping some of the reserves motivated and positive due to a lack of playing time. I shared with him something I had learned from a former coach: Often it is not the number of minutes, but the opportunity to play significant minutes that matters the most and keeps the spirit vibrant. Our coach called to the end of the bench for Bob to enter the game. The student section erupted into a wild frenzy, and they began to chant Bob's name. What happened next not only influenced the outcome of the game (we went on to stretch our halftime lead and win the game), but it also gave everyone a sense of hope that, at any moment, any moment any one of them could be called on to have their chance to shine in a game that mattered.

In a mere forty-six seconds, Bob secured a defensive rebound, scored a basket the first time down the court on a post feed from a teammate, took a charge on the defensive end, then grabbed an offensive rebound, scored on a put back, got fouled, and made the free throw. Each time Bob ran up and down the court, the smile on his face grew wider. When he snared the last defensive rebound of the half after a missed shot, Bob ran off the court with the energy and spirit of a championship winner, pumped his fists, and yelled with excitement. On that night, Bob finally believed he had contributed to his team's win and felt a sense of pride and accomplishment he had not experienced all season. All it took was for one coach to carry the banner for a player, giving him his signature moment Whether you are a coach, an elementary teacher, an orchestra instructor, or you serve as a middle school social studies teacher, the goal should be to empower your students to achieve their peak level of performance—not just in the heat of the moment, but every day. When we are at our best, our team benefits and our community flourishes.

Every child deserves the opportunity to be a part of something great! I am often reminded of the words of the late Rita Pierson, a former Texas teacher and administrator: "Every student deserves a champion, an adult who will never give up on them, who understands the power of connection and insists they become the best they can possibly be." Yes, our students deserve for us to expect their best! They also deserve for us to bring our best, to be crazy about them, to believe in them, and to inspire them in new ways. As educators, we should all aspire to help transform our students' lives, and the best way to do that is to allow them to be part of a community that expects their very best. My hope is that all students will have an opportunity to look back on their school experience and cherish the memory of caring adults who believed in them, pushed them toward excellence, gave them their chance (sometimes several) to "have their moment," and carried their banner in their hearts. What an amazing gift we have been given to be able to touch the deepest part of a child's heart!

Eyes on Culture by Danny Steele

**Principal, Thompson Sixth Grade Center,
Alabaster City Schools, Birmingham, Alabama**

As a principal, it is always my goal to carry the banner for our school. I want to lead by example. I want to articulate a vision that inspires our students and empowers our teachers. And I hope to rally everyone in the building in a collective pursuit of that vision with me. While we are relentless in our efforts at raising student achievement, we remain mindful that, ultimately, our work is centered around the kids.

At the beginning of this school year, we asked all our students to write their dreams on our "Wall of Dreams," and we asked all our staff members to write their hopes for our students on the wall outside our main office. These hopes and dreams remind us each day of the reasons we come to work, and they remind us what we're about—making a difference for kids. I talk about this at faculty meetings, at Open House, at PTO meetings, and anytime I am escorting visitors around our building. I strive to ensure that there is never any ambiguity about our purpose or our passion. Our mission can be found in my emails to staff, in my tweets, and in my blogs. We are about the kids, and it is my goal that this message is consistently communicated in and around the school.

We demonstrate every day, through what we say and through how we spend our time, that meeting the needs of our students is the most important thing we do. We work tirelessly to connect with our students, to advocate for them, and to ensure they have the support they need to succeed. And we remind our staff that they are leaving a legacy that transcends the curriculum: We are creating a brighter future for our children.

I Would Never Want Your Job

Through the years, I have participated in dozens (if not hundreds) of conversations with teachers, students, parents, principals, and aspiring administrators about the challenges that come with being an educator. The conversations often lead me to reflect on the work that building leaders do daily and to determine what it is exactly that causes others to say, "I would never want your job."

The truth is, I worry about the long-term impact made by the perception that is often associated with the work we do. These perceptions could lead potential principal and teacher candidates to believe that being an educator is not worth the effort, time, and energy. One way to combat this perception is to ask people who say, "I would never want your job" why they feel that way—and then address their concerns and misconceptions. Even educators can fall into the trap of agreeing with negative comments about working in the school system or with children, and that can give "outsiders" the impression that we are somehow special or can manage so much more than others because we work with children. Yes, it takes a caring and devoted person to be a teacher or administrator, but we are not superhuman! Sure, we handle challenges daily, but quite frankly, so do counselors, secretaries, school nurses, social workers, and the support staff members who work in schools.

We need to change some of the perceptions that cause people to believe teaching and school administration roles are not worth the challenge. We need people of excellence leading in our classrooms, and we need the best classroom teachers to pursue administrative roles in schools so they can use their talents to make an even greater impact on our school communities. If you are a teacher and are wondering whether it's worth the risk and challenge to move into school leadership, or if you know a young person who is wondering whether education is the right career path, the answer is yes!

Here are a few of my thoughts on why others should aspire to be educators and school administrators:

- **You don't have to do it all by yourself.** The key to success is recognizing that everyone in your organization has strengths, skills, and talents. If cultivated, these abilities can help move your school forward in an efficient and positive manner. Building and being part of a strong, cohesive culture is one of the best parts about working in a school environment.

- **You don't have to have all the answers.** You have access to the collective knowledge and wisdom of dozens of other staff members who can help you navigate difficult issues. Leaning on others and asking for help can be invigorating for you and your staff. This will show your colleagues that you trust them and believe in their skills and abilities.

- **Even if you move into school leadership, you don't have to miss the kids.** Leaving the classroom doesn't have to mean you can't make the same type of impact with students that you made when you were a teacher. Creating your own opportunities for fostering positive and meaningful relationships with kids by seeking them out and spending time with them in intentional ways can still occur, and it is still unbelievably rewarding.

- **As an educator or principal, you can ensure your students have a voice.** What a tremendous opportunity we have, helping students share their voices and their talents!

When you are willing to invest in others and perform your responsibilities at a high level of excellence—regardless of your title—you will experience the truth firsthand that your role in education is not about a title but about making a significant difference in your colleagues' and students' lives. Refresh your mindset so you see the role of teacher or principal as a way of life, not as a job or a title. This will pay great dividends when it comes to staying positive and experiencing the joy of serving others. You'll discover, too, that every challenge can be an opportunity to grow and that many challenges really are a matter of perception. For example, the perception that some people have about building principals is that they spend all their time sitting in meetings or at their desks doing paperwork, answering emails, addressing naughty kids, or dealing with unreasonable parents. The reality is, the life of a principal can be full, exciting, and rewarding! As leaders, we must accept the responsibility to make our roles what we want them to become.

> ## Refresh your mindset so you see the role of teacher or principal as a way of life, not as a job or a title.

As you carry the banner for your school, consider how others (inside and outside of your school) see your role as an educator. We must realize that what others believe about what our job demands is also on us. It's up to each school leader and teacher to avoid getting stuck in a closed mindset that defines our roles as, "It is what it is, and it's always been this way." If our intentions are to inspire others to follow our lead and pursue a career in education, we must learn to tell our stories in a way that truly reflects how wonderful this profession is. Educators play a significant role in the lives of children and have the power to impact entire communities. My goal is to get people to stop saying, "I would never want your job," and start asking, "Who wouldn't want to be an educator?"

Carrying the banner means we take pride in our job. It also means we become advocates for how these jobs are important to the fabric of both our local and global communities and how they help us change the narrative of education to the public.

Carry the Banner

Educators who are personally and genuinely invested in others understand that their contributions carry beyond a positive voice by lifting others up and filling their cups with kindness and gratitude, inspiring others to want to do the same. They are committed to carrying the banner for their school community, always believing they can make a positive impact on everyone they meet. It is important to take time to surround yourself with others who help keep you focused on the things that matter, who energize you, and give you hope. Don't dwell on the negative or what isn't working. Forgetting or neglecting to rely on your teams—those who are in the best position to influence your beliefs, attitudes, voices, and behaviors—only compounds the problem. You must allow yourself the opportunities to be influenced in positive ways by your peers if you aim to inspire others to be impacted by your words, your beliefs, your actions, and your enthusiasm for this wonderful profession we call teaching.

> **It is important to take time to surround yourself with others who help keep you focused on the things that matter, who energize you, and give you hope.**

So ask yourself, *Am I carrying the banner for my students, colleagues, and school community every day, even on the days when nothing seems to go right?* If you do not bring that positive voice, how can you expect the same from others? I challenge you to infuse a sense of pride into every conversation and every action and to be intentional about inspiring others to want to do the same.

CULTURE BUILDER #1

The 10-Minute Collaborative Model—Many of the educators I have encountered are what I call "fixers." They love to fix problems. This isn't necessarily a bad quality to have, and they generally have the best of intentions. The problem comes when the burden of solving every problem falls on your shoulders because others see that you relish the role of fixer. Rather than working to find a solution themselves, people will hand you the problem to deal with time and time again.

Whether you are a classroom teacher or a building administrator, your effectiveness as a problem solver and decision maker will be greater if you use a collaborative approach that allows the ideas, experiences, and perspectives of others to support both you and them in resolving issues. This model can also be used as a way to change a good idea into an excellent one that has the greatest impact possible on a change of practice. Here is an approach that I have seen used efficiently and effectively by teachers and administrators:

- Gather a group of four or five people to resolve an issue or improve upon an idea or process.

- Take one minute to share the problem or idea. The rest of the group members are to listen only.

- Group members get two minutes to ask clarifying questions for more information. The presenter writes down questions. (Important to note that group members are not to offer suggestions or ideas of their own at this time; this is strictly a time to only ask questions.)

- The presenter gets two minutes to respond to questions. Again, group members only listen.

- Group members then get two minutes to rapidly fire ideas and suggestions to support the work of the presenter. The presenter quickly jots down the new ideas shared.

- All group members now get three minutes to dive deeper into new ideas presented, followed by more clarifying questions and comments from all group members to help craft the original issue or idea to a level of excellence.

The strict structure and time limits in this process reinforce a couple of valuable qualities from which we can all benefit when it comes to working collaboratively with others. First, it helps us develop our listening skills. Too often we want to jump right in and try to resolve an issue or generate a new idea before we really have time to digest the original concept or problem. Second, it reminds us of the truth behind the unconference model that the smartest person in the room is the room. Use this approach and watch how, in ten minutes, you can resolve an issue or improve upon an idea or process while building a stronger capacity for your organization and you.

CULTURE BUILDER #2

Acknowledging vs. Ignoring Inappropriate Student Behavior— As an educator, you are going to come across situations where you hear certain things or observe inappropriate behaviors that do not meet the high standards to which your school is trying to hold its students. Conversations or behaviors that are deemed inappropriate for the school environment should not go unaddressed.

Even if you don't know the student, engage him or her as if you do. In other words, set the standard of expectation that all students in the school are *your* students. Some educators believe that addressing students who aren't "theirs" is not their job; they feel it's the job of administration to deal with discipline problems outside their classrooms. My perspective is that everyone is responsible for carrying the banner for their school community at all times, and that means being willing to acknowledge, either through words or actions (and always in a respectful tone and manner), that certain behaviors are not acceptable in the school environment. This sends a clear and consistent message that everyone will be held to the same high standard.

CULTURE BUILDER #3

Telling Your School's Story—Co-authors of *The Power of Branding*, Joe Sanfelippo (@Joe_Sanfelippo), superintendent of Fall Creek School District in Wisconsin, and Tony Sinanis (@TonySinanis), superintendent of Hastings-on-Hudson district in New York, often share that if the story of your school is being told by people who don't have a connection to it, then you probably need to change your approach. Here are some ways to share your story and tell the world about all the great things going on in your school:

- **Create a district hashtag.** Think of this hashtag as a community where your students, staff, alumni, and school community come together with pride to share all the great things going on in your school or district. Select one hashtag for your entire district rather than a different hashtag for each individual school. The premise here is to build one community that is unified where everyone can visit. It also has a better chance of being more active, which will entice people to visit it and tag it more. Use this same hashtag for every celebration, event, training, in-service, conference, etc. Think *one community*.

- **Create multiple school accounts.** To personalize messages for specific schools, grade levels, clubs, or classrooms, create multiple social media accounts on Twitter, Facebook, Instagram, etc. to get others to highlight their specific programs, such as Fine Arts, Athletics, Clubs/Organizations, Student Voice, Administration, and Parent Booster Organizations. Encourage them to tag the district hashtag when tweeting.

- **Link all your social media accounts.** This makes it easy to push out tweets along with Facebook, Instagram, Flickr, Tumblr, or Pinterest posts simultaneously on multiple platforms.

- **Link all your social media apps to your district website.** When families are new to your community, your district and school websites are among the first places they go to find information on your district and to help them decide which school to attend. Make it easy for them to connect with your school community by providing all your social media information in one place.

- **Promote and post your school hashtag and social media accounts** on your stationery, newsletters, website, note cards, business cards, signage, scoreboards, etc. around campus. Brand, brand, brand.

- **Use your television monitors around school/campus to stream tweets, hashtags, Facebook posts, etc., in real time.** This is where school leaders hesitate for fear of negative postings being seen by the school community. Understand that students and others do not need your permission to post negative comments and are already doing so. Making content visible brings these issues to the forefront and allows you to address concerns. We cannot hide from the dissenters, nor should we. When you see a negative comment, consider it an opportunity to build or repair relationships.

- **Provide open access.** Again, many oppose this idea, worried that students and staff will spend most of their time perusing social media, checking their feeds, and posting their comments rather than focusing on school and learning. If this is the case, then shouldn't we begin to question why students are not engaging in our lessons and school in general? Have we created an environment that is so disinteresting that they have no desire to focus on their own learning?

- **Inspire others to connect**. Don't mandate that students and teachers use social media applications; instead, inspire them to invest in social media connection by showing them its benefits and helping them see how their interaction online could support them in their learning and teaching. Model its use at every gathering, whether it be faculty meetings, in-service trainings, parent meetings, or student assemblies by having your social media accounts streaming live and demonstrating the benefits, resources, and connections that can be gained from these tools. Telling our schools' stories and bringing about change in a digital era begins with us, so let's embrace the digital world of technology and begin to find ways to use it to tell our story.

ARE YOU...

KILLING   or   BUILDING

they   we
gossip   defend
always done this way   dare to be different
isolate   collaborate
awfulize   inspire

CULTURE?

School communities that are rich in tradition and that honor both their past and present students and staff understand that by investing in each other, they are ultimately investing in their own identity as a school community. They are inherently carrying the banner for a cause greater than themselves. These passionate educators have a strong desire to impact their schools and school districts in a favorable way and understand that positive energy equals synergy that can permeate the organization. They are selfless in their actions and focus their efforts and their energy first on filling the cups of others. They also recognize the value of refilling their own cup after they have first taken care of their colleagues. Through their unselfish actions, they can discern the benefits that come with seeing their work from a life-fit perspective and mentally and emotionally bring a better and more invested approach to their work with students. By doing so, they become Future Ready, not just focusing on the learning gaps of their students but also gaining a better understanding of the opportunity gaps that exist. They'll see ways they can address these gaps in a pro-active, collaborative way as opposed to thinking they have to resolve these gaps in isolation. For this reason, they can advocate for the advantages their profession provides, especially when others begin to question and make comments that suggest they would never want their job as an educator. This is why educators, regardless of the number of years they have served as a teacher or served in schools, find themselves still wanting to be inspired.

Your students and colleagues need you to remain invigorated and eager to come to work every day, the same way you did on your first day. Our profession doesn't need more culture killers. It needs you to be a culture builder. You choose how you want to approach each day, so carry the banner in a positive way by bringing a positive voice to every conversation and every interaction. By doing so, you will leave the campus a better place than when you arrived.

QUESTIONS FOR DISCUSSION

- What strategies can you use to respond to those in your organization who are negative or speak disparagingly about others—without alienating them?

- What can you do as an educator to give yourself a reprieve when things are not going well?

- What are some things you or your team can start doing today to help support life-fit so that everyone is at their best?

- What can we do to encourage the growth of teachers and leaders to inspire people to move into education and/or into school leadership?

CHAPTER 5

CORE PRINCIPLE 4:
Be a Merchant of Hope

*It's one thing to say we have high
expectations for kids... but another
to say I will be here to help you... no
matter your struggles!*

—Salome Thomas-EL

The fourth core principle that distinguishes a culturized school is that its educators serve as merchants of hope. These educators know it is their responsibility to ignite a spark in the culture that allows every student and every staff member to be a part of something great. The goal is to create a culture where the members of the school community feel as if no limits are placed on their talents or strengths and where their dreams to achieve the impossible can be realized.

I still remember the first visit I ever made to a student's home. I was a teacher in the Milwaukee Public School system, and making the home visit was not my idea. My assistant principal, Mr. Leonard, had asked me to join him on a home visit. A few days prior, I had expressed my displeasure with Mr. Leonard about the way he handled a disciplinary matter with an eighth-grade boy named Michael who swore at me in front of my entire class. I wanted him suspended for his behavior, and I wanted him removed from my class. Michael was a "difficult student." Long before the incident in my classroom, I had heard from several teachers that he was "not going to make it" because he didn't care about school.

We drove down a street lined with run-down houses as we approached Michael's home. A few of the homes had boards on the windows, while others were covered with plastic. The sagging porches on so many of the houses looked as though they could cave in at any moment. I remember the sight of empty cans strewn across the edge of the road. Broken bottles and trash filled the yards. Kids played in the street, riding bikes and kicking cans. A few girls jumped rope while a few gentleman sat on a porch and yelled at their neighbors across the way. Every now and then a car would drive by with loud music. As we got out of the car, I heard a horn honk, and somebody yelled out to the kids, "Get out of the street before you get hit by a car!"

Mr. Leonard was a good man who loved kids, and the kids loved and respected him. It was easy to see how much they enjoyed being around him. I liked him, too, and would often talk with him about his job as an administrator. He told me more than once that there were days in which he wanted to walk away from it—that the job seemed impossible. But then he would quickly share how he couldn't leave his kids. He would often say, "I feel these kids need me. I want to make sure they are given a fair chance and treated right. If we don't take time to get to know them, who will? For many of our kids, school is the only place they feel safe." Seeing Michael's neighborhood put that last comment into a new light for me.

Mr. Leonard called in through the screen door, "Mrs. Smith? Michael, anybody home?" A small old lady came to the door. Opening it, she smiled at Mr. Leonard and said, "It is so good to see you again." I will never forget the warm embrace I saw Mrs. Smith give Mr. Leonard that day. It was clear that Mr. Leonard had formed a special bond with Michael's grandmother. As they talked for the next thirty minutes, I learned that Mr. Leonard had visited Michael's home several times since Michael's mother had passed. Michael's grandmother shared that Mr. Leonard was more than a principal to Michael; he was like a father.

As we walked back to the car, I curiously asked Mr. Leonard how long Michael had lived with his grandmother. He suddenly stopped and turned around. "You need to know something, Mr. Casas. Michael has lived with his grandmother the last two years. His mother died in a house fire two years ago. Michael and his brothers were playing with matches one night and the house caught on fire, killing his mother and two siblings. Michael has never been the same since."

Mr. Leonard's words left me momentarily paralyzed. How could I have been so focused on myself that I didn't know this about Michael? Why hadn't I taken the time to get to know him? How had I not known this? I felt like a failure. As we drove away, tears streamed down my face as I thought of how it would feel to lose my own parents.

Many years later, I sat in my office looking at grade reports and was astonished by the number of failing grades of many of our freshman students. *How could this be?* I wondered. *What more could we do to reduce the number of failures among our ninth graders?* At a loss for immediate answers, I let those questions stew in my mind until, while at a conference with my guidance team a couple weeks later, we were asked to create and implement a plan to monitor student progress and collect data. Initially, we tossed around the idea of monitoring standardized tests, but none of us could get excited about that. Then I remembered the grade reports that I had reviewed and suggested to my team that we monitor incoming ninth graders who were considered as high risk based on their academic performance in eighth grade. Remembering Michael and his grandmother, I suggested that we explore the possibility of taking a proactive approach and visiting with the students and their families the summer before the start of high school. And just like that, we created the Home Visit Program.

When we returned to school after the conference, we didn't waste any time finalizing and implementing our action plan. We felt it was important for the counselors and administrators to team up and conduct the home visits together. We provided gift bags, visited with the students and families about their students' middle school experience, the positives and challenges of middle school, what they most looked forward to in high school, and what they were most concerned about. We talked about their interests, goals, and hopes for high school. In other words, we focused on making connections, establishing a foundation of trust, and laying out a plan for support. We hoped to gain some insight on how we could support our families so they could become advocates for their children and help them succeed as they transitioned into high school. Although we all recognized that home visits were not a novel idea, it gave our families and our staff an avenue for communication. Ultimately, we wanted to create a sense of hope that together we could provide a positive environment where the students felt valued and safe. The personal connections we made with these students and their families were the first step toward making a positive difference in the lives of these students who had been identified as high-risk.

Picking up the Pieces

When it comes to working with students on an individual basis, I often think back on my days in Milwaukee. I learned so much from the wisdom of strong leaders like Mr. Leonard. My experiences in those early years in that urban setting shaped my thinking about the value of establishing meaningful relationships with the people around me. One of the most important lessons I learned is that to make those connections and build the kinds of relationships that make a difference, we need to take time to listen to and get to know our students on a personal and consistent basis.

One of the most successful strategies for connecting with students and developing trusting relationships is one I picked up during my first year as an associate principal from the principal who hired me. He modeled for me over and over the value and importance of following up with students a day or two after dealing with them in any type of discipline situation. After any disciplinary action, he would seek them out and ask them if they understood why he had disciplined them. He would listen to what the student had to say and then share with the student that it was because he had high expectations for them and cared about them. He would often say something like, "I never want you to think it is okay to behave in that manner. I have higher expectations for you than that. I am always going to encourage you to look at your own behavior and ask yourself what you did to contribute to the situation." He would then make it a point to search out the student—in the hallway during a passing period or in the cafeteria—and check in on them, ask how they were doing, compliment them in some capacity, share a personal story, etc. until a meaningful relationship had been established. The students learned that their principal cared about them personally—not just about correcting their mistakes.

To this day, I still use this strategy to connect with students and refer to it as "Picking up the Pieces." However, I modified my approach a bit and added these two simple questions immediately after all disciplinary discussions.

Do you feel I treated you fairly?

Do you think I care about you?

If I conducted myself appropriately and managed the conversation in a way that the student felt valued and that their voice was heard, the answer to those two questions would be a solid yes. If not, then I would have to be willing to accept the feedback and work even harder to build that trust.

This practice helped me learn that showing love and support for an individual doesn't mean you always agree with them. In fact, it often means telling them what they don't want to hear because it is the best way for them to reflect on their own behavior so growth can occur. In other words, it is important to ask students what role they played in impacting the situation in a negative way and to encourage them to take responsibility for their own conduct.

When I reflect on the interactions I had with my own students, I understand now that my negative experiences as a student helped me connect with the most challenging and troubled students. Furthermore, being of Mexican-American descent, it allowed me to relate to the personal struggles of students who felt they were being treated differently due to the color of their skin. Those personal experiences gave me some perspective on what my school's struggling learners were facing daily, and it gave me some insight on how to influence their behavior in a positive way. But please do not misunderstand having insight with having all the right answers. On the contrary, I know I have failed more often than I have succeeded. I often think of the Michael Jordan commercial where he shares that he missed over nine thousand shots, lost more than three hundred games, was entrusted with taking the game winning shot twenty-six times… and missed. He states, "I failed and failed time and time again, which is why I succeed." Like Michael Jordan, I entered every student interaction with the confidence and belief that I could and would make a difference in his or her life. I then made it a priority to connect over and over again in an intentional way in order to establish a meaningful relationship.

I have grown as a school leader and in managing student behavior as much through my mistakes as I have through my successes. When I became a school administrator at the age of twenty-six, I had so many ideas, philosophies, and thoughts on how to manage student behavior and establish relationships with young people. Looking back, I realize I tried to depend too much on my own personal struggles as a way to connect with students. Although our experiences were similar in many ways, there were also unique differences to every story that lent themselves to students losing confidence in a system that seemed not to care whether they succeeded or failed. Over time, I learned that my greatest impact came from spending time listening to their stories and helping them see something more in themselves. The lessons I learned and skills I developed from my time talking with students over the years remain strongholds today; many have had to be adjusted. One thing that has not changed is the realization that I am as passionate today about teaching and learning as I was when I first started student teaching. I'm equally as passionate about utilizing the opportunity to have a positive influence on young people and the staff with whom I work. Developing purposeful relationships with all students and colleagues serves as a grain of hope and gives meaning to my work and my life.

Eyes on Culture by Kelly Tenkely
Principal, Anastasis Academy, Centennial, Colorado

Too often we assume that being a merchant of hope in education leads to grand Hollywood moments where students are empowered to go against the status quo, rip up books, and stand on their desks claiming education as their own. In reality, it's in the small moments that we become the merchant of hope. It's the relationships we build, the times we slow down enough to really see our students. It's those moments that don't feel all that grand or important.

It is in the pauses that we become the merchant of hope.

It's in the pauses that we connect. We let students know that we see them, that we are there for them, that we believe they are worthy of our time and attention.

As a computer teacher, I saw 475 students each week for thirty-five minutes at a time. One of the things I strove for each year was learning every student's name as quickly as possible. I would drill myself by going into the hall as the kids were on their way to lunch so that I could say "hello" by name and give high fives as they passed by. It was in the first month of school when a straight line of first grade students paraded by, and I hurried out to say my hellos. Benton stopped when I said his name, and with wide-eyed wonder exclaimed, "Mrs. Tenkely, you know my name?!" I'm sure I laughed and said something to the effect of, "Of course I do buddy! I see you every week, and you LOVE computers." He told me that other than his classroom teacher, no one else knew him.

Benton hugged me tight right there in the hallway before rushing to catch up with the rest of his class. For Benton, my knowing his name meant that I knew him.

From that day forward, Benton stopped by my classroom every afternoon to ask if I had any new websites to show him. It became such a routine that his mom started picking him up from my classroom to give us a few extra moments to geek out together over my newest finds. Every day he asked if I was going to write a blog about the website I was showing him; he loved getting the first peek before it was shared with the rest of the world. Benton's mother regularly pulled me aside to thank me for seeing her son. "Benton can be a handful; he gets into trouble so much at school, but he still loves to come because he wants to see what new websites you might have for him."

Knowing a student's name wouldn't make a great plot for an Oscar-winning, Hollywood production. But it was in that small moment—the pause in the hall—that Benton felt known.

It is in those small quiet moments, the pauses, the ones we often overlook, that we become a merchant of hope. It is taking the time to see our students. To connect and know them by name.

Every Rose Has Its Thorns

Anyone who knows me well knows that I spent an extraordinary amount of time reflecting on my work when I was a principal. In fact, I reflected so much that I often chose thinking about work over choosing to sleep. (That's probably not a good thing, I know.) However, it wasn't so much the work I thought about but the people with whom and for whom I worked; the staff and students were constantly on my mind. More than anything, I wanted them to look forward to coming to school every day. I wanted them to feel valued, to believe that our administration genuinely cared about them, and to feel that we honored them for the contributions they brought to our school community every day. Early on in my teaching career, I would challenge myself to try and make an impact on my students in a favorable way with the hope that perhaps my influence on them would spill beyond the school day, and I would be the topic of conversation at the dinner table.

Through the course of my career, I have served in schools that were filled with both joy and challenges. As a building principal, I chose to focus daily on the joys of the job and reflect on how I could respond to the challenges in a positive way. I wanted to create an environment where people felt they could own their successes and failures, particularly when given the opportunity for self-reflection and self-change.

I recall a few years ago my associate principal explaining one of her family traditions to me. Her family would sit in a circle and share their "rose and thorn" stories for the day (or week or any length of time they chose for the discussion). We decided to incorporate this practice with our new teachers during our beginning- and end-of-year new teacher socials. As we wrapped up our final new teacher meeting one year, every one of us was given the opportunity to share our rose and our thorn story for the school year. Their willingness to own their moment when they were given the opportunity to reflect on the year and their thoughtful responses touched me. Their roses included colleagues that made them feel valued and welcomed. They expressed their gratitude for an administration that genuinely supported them. They shared their appreciation for a student-centered culture that focused on building strong relationships with students. I felt a sense of joy when I heard their responses, even when they followed up their roses with their thorns. They spoke of personal experiences that included feeling fatigued at the end of each day, working with challenging students, a desire for classroom windows, difficulty managing the workload, and the overwhelming feeling that every new teacher experiences in their first year. However, what brought me the most joy that afternoon was that each thorn was quickly followed by another rose, in almost an apologetic manner. How refreshing it was to listen to our teachers respond to their challenges by focusing on the positives that came from being poked by a bristle on a stem. Without hesitation, they chose to own their experiences by shifting their focus to the petals on the rose rather than the thorn on the stem.

For the most part, those bristles often come in the form of our most challenging students. Yet every now and then we are reminded that many of our students who remain closed buds during their school years often blossom into beautiful roses long after they leave us. I have been blessed numerous times by the emotional high of re-connecting with students whose petals had wilted during their school years as we desperately tried to care for them. If you have ever watched a kid spiral downward right in front of you, you know the raw emotion of those moments when you blame yourself for not being able to help a student detour his or her path of self-destruction. It is heartbreaking to watch talented and beautiful young students fall victim to drug addiction, sexual abuse, homelessness, theft, prison, and hopelessness. But when those lost or hurting children return to your office years later as adults who are full of life, laughter, and a new-found hope, the emotion is just as powerful, and those feelings of regret are replaced with joy. In my own career, some of those visits have included a young mother who found freedom from sexual assault and addiction and gave birth to a beautiful baby. She was a soon-to-be wife, working and attending college and building a happy life. Another example is a young man free from prison with a second chance at life who enrolled in college and began working to help others avoid the mistakes he had made. And finally, a young man who overcame his demons of drug abuse and criminal activity to return home to the unconditional love and support of his family and begin a new life, working and planning to enroll in college.

Each one of them is a beautiful rose on a stem full of thorns. Each one of them has a future full of beautiful petals. Each one of them owning their successes and failures. And I am so thankful to have had the chance to see it.

How We Respond Is Our Choice

Granted, when all your students are well behaved and your school district has plenty of money for the kinds of activities and programs you want to explore, modeling a kind, positive, excellence-focused mindset isn't terribly difficult. But let's get real. Most educators work in time-crunched, less-than-perfect conditions. In our line of work, every day brings new challenges. Money is almost always spread too thinly across too few teachers, and students come into our schools and classrooms with all manner of needs, wounds, and issues that can tie us up and slow us down. When (not if) you're dealing with frustrating situations, remember that even though you can't choose your circumstances or the students on your roster, you can decide the kind of climate you will create by being intentional about your response to those situations. How you respond to them is always a choice.

I was working late one night clearing up a pile of paperwork on my desk that had snuck up on me in a period of just three days. As often happened to me when I was organizing my desk, I got side-tracked. I came across a stack of paperwork for early graduate students that needed to be signed, and as I began to examine each student record closely, my mind wandered a bit. Instead of rejoicing in the fact that these students had met the criteria for early graduation, I started thinking about the students who had given up and quit school in previous years. I immediately began to pull up their pictures on our student information system so I could look at their faces again. In doing so, their needs became personal to me. As their principal, I couldn't help but feel I had not done enough. After an hour or so of stewing on what I wished I'd done, I sent out the following tweets on my Twitter account:

> **"Reflecting on why we don't reach every HS student. Feel like I need to do more. Plan 2 call kids this week who have given up." #stillhavehope**

> **"Challenge to my administrative PLN. Call 3 kids this week who either quit/plan 2 quit school & be their hope. Let's be the change 2gether."**

At one time or another, every educator hides behind the line, "I don't have time to...." The hard truth is that we determine what we have time for—and what we don't have time for. When something matters a great deal to us, we find a way to make time. In this case, making the time to call students who had dropped out netted five students returning to school. Like the starfish story, we may not have reached all of them, but we made a difference to a few. In turn, they made an impact on our lives, inspiring us to continue to connect with students who have given up.

Shortly after this experience, I had an interaction with a student who wanted to quit school. I was coming off the high of five students returning to school, and now I was in danger of losing one to the streets of what I call "lost hope." As we spoke, I shared a quote by Thomas Paine: "The harder the conflict, the more glorious the triumph," I told him. I wanted him to see beyond his current internal conflict and believe that the turmoil he felt could evolve into an experience that would allow him to grow and find his greater purpose. In the end, I explained that he had the power to write his own story. And because of that power, he wasn't doomed or destined to fail or give up. In other words, how he responded could help define his triumph. It took ongoing support, much patience, and time invested—by the student, his teachers, counselor, and our dean of students. We were able to work with his mother and get him back on the right path, eventually helping him earn his diploma and reminding us once again that we can be the change our kids sometimes long for.

That's a lesson for all of us. Remaining positive daily starts with recognizing that the way we choose to respond to our circumstance defines us. This is true for administrators, teachers, secretaries, classroom aides, kitchen staff, special needs support staff, custodians, bus drivers, and parent volunteers. We have the power to choose, and one way to ensure better choices it to take time to reflect on what we're doing out of habit and then course correct as needed. Here are ten ways you can challenge yourself to choose a positive response and be a merchant of hope for all students:

1. **Bring your best to work every day.** Be grateful you get the opportunity to make a positive impact on a child every day!

2. **Give two minutes of your time to one student and one staff member every day.** Be intentional with your time and

then follow up with a quick word or note. The small things can make all the difference.

3. **Be empathetic.** Taking the time to understand, share, and be sensitive to another person's feelings is critical in building a culture of trust.

4. **Value the mistakes of others.** Risk takers are born here. If you yourself make a mistake, own it, apologize, ask for forgiveness and work to make sure it doesn't happen again.

5. **Model forgiveness.** If you want to be an effective leader, be willing to sincerely accept an apology and move on. Believe that most people's intentions are good.

> # If you want to be an effective leader, be willing to sincerely accept an apology and move on. Believe that most people's intentions are good.

6. **Understand you will not always see immediate results when working with kids.** Be patient and think long term. Many "troubled" students are just testing a system which has failed them many times over long before you came into the picture.

7. **Have high standards for all kids every day.** Do not make excuses for kids based on race, socio-economic class, environment, poor parenting, etc. Believe in all kids all the time. (It also helps if you love them all the time too!)

8. **Address inappropriate behavior.** When you don't address inappropriate behavior, you send a message that the students or staff in question are not worth the effort and/or that you have given up. If you hesitate to correct poor behavior because you are worried about their response to you, you have become part of the problem.

9. **Don't be negative.** Constant complaining and speaking negatively about kids, staff, work environment, etc. without offering a solution is a poorer reflection on you than those about whom you are complaining. Bring positive energy every day.

10. **Take time to smile/laugh and encourage others to have fun.** When it is no longer fun to go to work, it is time to do something else.

For me, the things that keep me up at night are the same things that get me up in the morning charged and ready to go to work. Sure, there are challenges, but those challenges bring opportunity. Every day can be great if we choose to make it great. We are not going to be able to control everything that happens to us every day, but we can control how we allow it to affect us. This quote by American composer Irving Berlin sums it up best: "Life is ten percent of what you make it. The other ninety percent is how you take it." We are the only ones with the power to choose our own response. It is our duty to be a positive voice for every child, every teacher, every day.

> ## "Life is ten percent of what you make it. The other ninety percent is how you take it."

Eyes on Culture
by Kimberly Hurdhorst

**Science Teacher, Innovation Academy Westwood
Middle School, Spring Lake Park, Minnesota**

As a teacher, staff member, or an administrator, it is vital to be a merchant of hope. We can do this by honoring the stories people want to tell by authentically listening and by creating spaces for that speaking and listening to flourish. I myself find that Genius Hour and teaching students to harness the power of hope through speaking and listening skills as they prepare to give their own TED Talks creates a learning legacy because I am letting students know that they are born for significance. I do this with intentionality as I remind them that their purpose is wrapped up in both their passions and their compassion and to give hope to others.

Hope is a gift received as well as a gift returned to the world.

This was never clearer to me during the school year of 2015-2016 when I was a third-grade teacher. First Trimester of that year, I had Neva in the beginning hiding under the table with oceans of tears pouring from her eyes because she was terrified to speak in public. She eventually learned to apply our only class rule, BE BRAVE to overcome fear, and by the end of the trimester, she was able to speak with a friend by her side in the classroom to present her genius hour projects to just her classmates. I had hope, and through careful selection of books that were about prevailing and TED Talks about overcoming, she was able to lean in more to her brave core as we practiced our genius hour strategies, practiced public speaking skills, and listened to TED Talks that were given by youth on innovation and creativity. Neva emerged in front of her own classmates bravely by herself, and though she was timid, she was able to stand with her new genius hour project.

As we entered our third trimester, it was her turn to speak from the heart. We had spent the whole year learning that genius is a combination of your passions and your compassion. With strong confidence under her feet boosted by encouragement from me, all her classmates, and her family, she stood in front of fifty people to share from her heart how she would be the change in the world, though she was only in grade three. To do it, she was going to coach children on what to do when they are being bullied and show love by teaching people to knit. Her heart was full because, to do this, she had to push past her fears in which her speech impediment had previously bound her. Through the middle of the storm, she found hope and made it to the other side. Her parent's eyes were full of tears of love and I was insanely proud of her. Her parents remembered the first time she hid, the first time she cried, the first time she failed but tried again and here she was, tall and radiant, bold and confident. Neva ran for student council the following year in fourth grade with an address to her class, and though she didn't win, she tried. That is the miracle that hope gives you. It takes you back to the place where you heard hope first call your name, and you remember the first rule of life: Be Brave and Try Again.

The Most Important Gift

I am not embarrassed to admit I can get emotional and cry easily when I am watching or sharing a story that tugs at my heart. I have been known to shed a tear or two during a sad movie, a faculty meeting, celebrating a student's achievement during a recognition program, or speaking to other educators about my personal life journey. Most often my tears come from the joy I get from others when they share a personal story or take time to give me a compliment about some small impact I made on them during a period of self-doubt.

In 2014, I returned from a conference inspired and full of hope, but for more reasons than you might think. Yes, I was moved once again by the inspirational words of outstanding professionals in our field who gave me hope. I was touched and emotionally moved by conversations with teachers and leaders whom I both respect and admire and who, over the years, have become genuine friends and confidants. Yet surprisingly it was the generosity and gentle nature of one man who literally moved me to tears in the front seat of a shuttle van.

His name was Rodd Jackson.

Rodd was working the evening shift for Hampton Hotel when Colin Wikan (@ColinWikan), my former colleague and dean of students at the time, and I stepped onto the shuttle that would take us to Turner Field for the Braves/Mets game. Immediately, Rodd greeted us with a wide smile and asked us where we were headed. "To the Omni hotel," I shared. "No problem, be glad to take you," he said. "Let me first take these folks for a nice pasta dinner, and then I will get you to the Omni." As we drove down the road, Colin and I tried to make friendly small talk with the other guests in the shuttle until Rodd informed us that they were Russian and did not speak any English. As I sat there, I watched in admiration as Rodd attempted to communicate to these folks for the next ten to fifteen minutes with so much sincerity, respect, and patience that, for a moment, I thought to myself how this gentleman of forty-two years should be in a classroom teaching somewhere. After all, his caring and sincere disposition alone would touch the heart of any student, parent, or guest who entered a classroom or school. When we finally arrived at the restaurant, he rushed around quickly to open the door and assisted in getting them to the right entrance of the restaurant. He jumped back into the vehicle energized to assist us, his next customers, to our destination. How refreshing it was to hear Rodd talk about the Russian guests in such a positive light as he drove down the road. Had it been a cab driver who had shuttled them, he would have been cursing them all the way back to the station (based on our experience with Atlanta cab drivers that week). As he drove, Rodd engaged Colin and me in conversation the entire time. But this was different. There was a tender tone and genuine sincerity in his voice as he spoke to us. Suddenly, he asked me how long I had been a principal. "Twenty years," I said. "Wow, that's a long time. You must really love what you do," he responded. "How long until you retire," he asked. "I love what I do, so probably never," I said.

What Rodd asked me next completely caught me off guard. "How many students have come back to tell you thank you for making a difference in their lives? he asked. "Two," I responded in a joking manner. As I tried to think about his question in my head, I thought to myself, *Now, that is what our world should be all about: making a difference.* I laughed and rescinded my initial response with, "Who knows? Hundreds. Maybe even thousands because I have been at it a long time." As I turned to look at him still wondering why he had asked such a question, a look of sadness and despair had come over his face, and I could tell his eyes were watered. "I wish I would have gotten a chance to tell my high school principal thank you," he said. "He was the one who believed in me and helped me to graduate from high school. I cared more about partying and avoiding work than I did studying, but he stayed on me. He would often ask me when I was acting out if how I was behaving was appropriate. I still remember that because, as I got older, I figured it out. And you know what? He was right." "It's never too late," I said. "Why don't you just call him and let him know?" I asked. "Because he passed away," said Rodd. He went on to share that he had told his principal's children and his widow how much he had meant to him, but he couldn't help but share once again that he wished he could have told his principal personally how much he admired him and taught him about life. He wished he could tell him that he went to college and graduated with a degree in Interior Design. He wanted him to be proud of him. "I am sure it meant a lot to them that you took the time to tell them the impact he had on you," I said. "They truly appreciated your kind gesture and hearing about the impact he made on you and others, I am sure." As we pulled into our destination, I could feel my eyes welling up with tears. Rodd had touched my inner core with his heartfelt story about his principal. As he drove off, all I could think about was my hope and desire to make that kind of impact on my students so someday they might share with a complete stranger the kind of impact I had made on them. Honestly, I wished we had not arrived so quickly to the hotel because I wanted to keep talking to Rodd so I could learn more about his story.

Within ten minutes I realized I had made a mistake and had gone to the wrong hotel where we were meeting friends who had planned to take us to the game. Eventually, Colin and I made our way back outside with the idea of hailing a cab to the game. As we walked out of the CNN building, several cabs were heading in the opposite direction. In the middle of traffic, a shuttle van stopped, the window rolled down, and a man hollered at us. It was Rodd. I ran across the street and explained to him that I had erred and that we were now going to have to take a cab ride to Turner Field. "Hurry up, get in," he said. "Are you sure?" I said, "You are going in the wrong direction." Rodd called back, "It's no problem, I will take care of you." I yelled for Colin, and we both jumped into the back seat. "I thought you couldn't travel that far out of your perimeter," I said. "I can't," he stated, "but I will take you to the shuttle area, and they will drop you off right in front of the stadium." And this he did.

Let me just say this world needs more people like Rodd Jackson. Admittedly, there are days when I wish I had a million dollars. Not so I could go out and purchase a new car or buy a bigger house or even hire my own personal chef to cater to my love for food. Nope. I wish I had that kind of money so I could fly the Rodds of the world to my parent's house and give them a gift from my heart: a taste of my mama's home cooking. It would be like *Undercover Boss*—you know, the show that features the experiences of senior executives working undercover in their own companies to investigate how their firms really work and to identify how they can be improved, as well as to reward hard-working employees like Rodd. At the end, the executives return to their true identity and request the employees they identify to travel to a central location—often corporate headquarters (in this case, my mama's house). The bosses reveal their identity and reward hard-working employees through promotion or financial rewards.

At the time, I hoped and prayed that the executives at the Hampton/ Hilton Hotels realized and took the time to recognize Rodd for the value and the pride he brought to his work every day (maybe even fly him to corporate headquarters to personally thank him). Knowing Rodd for the brief time I had, I would guess he would deny or reluctantly accept because, in his heart, it was not about him, but about his customers. For my part, I hoped I could thank Rodd in a different kind of way since I am not a millionaire. I called the Hampton when I got home, and I spoke to the assistant general manager (I also emailed all the Hampton executives and shared my personal experience with

Rodd). I expressed to them how much I appreciated Rodd and told them how fortunate they were to have someone of his caliber working for them for the last six years. I was also able to talk to Rodd directly and tell him how much he meant to me and the impact he'd had on me as a principal, even after twenty years. I also asked him if he was okay with me sharing this story and revealing his identity because schools, small businesses, and large companies alike need to know there are still people out there like Rodd Jackson who take tremendous pride in their work every day and who are the true catalysts for hope in this world.

Rodd Jackson touched my heart that day and reminded me to take a moment to say thank you to those who make us feel like we are the most important people in the world, the world according to Rodd, where generosity and service to others is the most important gift we can share with others.

What Makes You Stay?

One of the most challenging and heart-wrenching experiences happens when our school communities are faced with the loss of a student. No amount of schooling or advanced degrees can ever prepare you to deal with the sight of an empty chair at graduation. That

> **No amount of schooling or advanced degrees can ever prepare you to deal with the sight of an empty chair at graduation.**

feeling of sorrow and helplessness never goes away. In fact, each time a young life is taken from a school community, it can resurrect feelings that have been harbored away since the last time such an experience occurred. As teachers and leaders, sometimes the pain and feelings of guilt consume you because you begin to question what or anything you could have said or done differently to prevent such a tragic loss from occurring.

The job of an educator is difficult. In fact, it is extremely difficult. Over the course of my career as an educator, I have lost several students. I share this in hopes that it will help other educators out there who may be questioning themselves on whether they can manage the emotional toll that comes with being an educator. As I shared earlier in the book, over the years I watched countless teachers and principals give so much of themselves to other people's children that, by the time they arrived home, they had nothing left to give to their own children and families. Most school teachers and school administrators are extremely passionate about what they do, can't imagine themselves doing anything else, and truly, truly believe they can make a difference in the lives of others. They believe it to the very core of their being that they can and will make a difference, hoping that the difference they make and the mark they leave on others will be positive and, in some instances, even life-changing. They want to be able to say and do the right thing when the moment calls on them, but the truth is, you won't always get it right, and when you don't, there will be times when you won't get the benefit of the doubt that you feel you deserve. This can be especially hurtful when you feel you have given everything to serve your students, families, or staff in order to help and support them and then feel disparaged or even defamed as a result of your decision or action. In these darkest moments, no one would blame you for doubting and asking yourself, *Is it really all worth it? This quote by Edward B. Lewis got me through many dark* days, "*We define ourselves by the best that is in us, not the worst that has been done to us.*"

Regardless of the number of times you are tested in your daily work as an educator, I hope you take the time in these moments to focus on the abundance of blessings rather than on scarcity or frustrations. I want to provide an encouraging word from someone who lived your life every day as a classroom teacher and a building administrator for more than twenty-five years, who experienced those same feelings you experience daily, whether they be feelings of joy, sorrow, gratification, accomplishment, frustration, or even doubt. My hope is that by taking the necessary time to reflect on the thoughts below, you will proceed forward and further than you ever thought possible.

Doubt is a part of being an educator. No doubt comes without a purpose. In your most challenging moments, lean on those you trust and let them know your biggest fears. Reaching out will strengthen your relationships with others and serve as a reminder that together you can prevail. Remember, alone you can be an example, but together, you can be exemplary!

See your wounds and pain as a symbol of strength, courage, and teachable moments. Don't be embarrassed or ashamed of them. See your resiliency in these challenges and ask yourself, *What am I learning about myself through this?* Take time to reflect on your journey so it can only get healthier and happier.

Keep going. No matter what, keep going. There will be times in your work when it feels like nothing can go right. Accept the fact that periodically your work as a teacher or leader is going to come at you hard. Sometimes you must go through difficult times in order to appreciate the best moments in your job. Some of your most critical learning comes from your biggest mistakes and most trying moments. Don't let these experiences discourage you; instead, cherish the challenges.

In many ways, my work as an educator has changed significantly in the last twenty-five years. In other ways, it has remained constant. The demands and pressures placed on teachers and school leaders today by parents, district personnel, and legislators at both the state and national levels are certainly greater than they have ever been, and not because you are asking for the attention, right? Yes, times are changing. So what can you do, moving forward? Start with believing that you can be the change our students deserve and no matter what, keep going. Is it really all worth it? I hope your answer to this question is yes. You see, our profession needs you. It needs you to not only tell your story but to keep living your story, even when you feel like you can't keep going.

What makes the most dedicated educators stick around? The same thing that got them in. The most effective educators didn't become a teacher or principal to help others be successful. They did it to change the environment and the conditions so they could have the best chance to be successful. We must take time to honor our teachers and principals for all that they do to make our schools a better place for all students by inspiring them to believe they can be more than they ever thought possible.

> **The most effective educators didn't become a teacher or principal to help others be successful. They did it to change the environment and the conditions so they could have the best chance to be successful.**

Be a Merchant of Hope

Educators who wish to leave a lasting legacy and their mark on their school community understand that, before they can transform teaching and learning, they must transform their belief systems. Believing that all students can be successful is no longer good enough, especially when our behaviors don't reflect what we are saying to others. Educators who last in this profession live in the long term versus the short term. They understand that long term allows them to maintain hope, whereas living in the short term often leads to frustration and giving up. Collectively, we can change the path of students' lives through our personal interactions with them, whether it be with a genuine smile, a sincere hello, or an intentional conversation to ask them how their day is going. Then take time to pause, listen, and follow up with a caring word of encouragement.

> **Educators who wish to leave a lasting legacy understand that, before they can transform teaching and learning, they must transform their belief systems.**

CULTURE BUILDER #1

Student Interviews—Commit to personally meeting with every student new to your classroom/school and ask them, "What do you love about your class/school? How is this class/school different than your last class/school? If you became the teacher/principal today, what is the first change you would make and why? What can I personally do to ensure your experience in this class/school is a positive one? " Nothing tells a new student that they are important more than taking the time to meet with them personally. What a positive experience this is for the student and for the staff member asking the questions! Listening to the responses of students who have transferred in from other school districts and sharing those responses with your staff will tell you a lot about your culture. The feedback you receive from your new students, I believe, will remind you of the importance of taking time to listen to your students' voices and creating a school climate where all students feel valued and respected and believe they matter. This activity can be done with students at any grade level. It's also just as effective and rewarding when done with staff. Include additional questions that align with your school's mission statement or school improvement plan to measure your success. To celebrate and recognize the hard work of your staff, take time to type up verbatim the student responses and share them with your team (use general themes to maintain confidentiality) during a staff meeting. Here are a few student reflections from such interviews:

"Surprised how easy it was to feel a part of the school even though I was new. I liked how much people welcomed me—both students and adults."

"Love it here. Teachers are much more helpful. I like the way they make themselves available. Students are a lot nicer here than in my old school."

"It is really big and thought it was going to be hard to meet people, but it has not been. Pretty cool. The teachers have been great and treat me like a young adult."

CULTURE BUILDER #2

Home Visit Mentor Program—Consider taking more of a proactive approach to supporting students and families who are struggling to find a connection or to achieve the success you had hoped for. Put into place a summer home visit mentor program. Be intentional in meeting with the adults in your school community who currently play a role or could play a role in supporting a stronger culture of family engagement. Put together a plan that includes the following:

1. Work with teachers/counselors/administrators from the transitioning grade/school to determine which students will be coming to you that are considered high risk based on past performance.
2. Select a set number of students and match them up with a teacher, counselor, and/or an administrator.
3. Determine partner teams, timelines, how to approach families, parent letters, schedules, talking points, meeting protocol, follow up check-ins, data collection, share out of information and recognition of students/families, etc.

4. Compile gift bags and items to be included, budgets, dona-
   tions, etc.

Prior to the start of the school year, contact families and schedule
the home visits. Partner up staff and have them conduct the home
visits together. Provide gift bags, visit with the student and family
about their student's prior experience, the positives and challenges
of that experience, ask what they most look forward to as they transition to a new grade/school, and what they are most concerned about.
Ask about their interests, their goals, and hopes for the upcoming
school year. In other words, focus on making a connection, setting
the foundation for trust, and establishing a plan for support. What
you are hoping to gain is some insight on how you can support your
families so they can become advocates for their children to help them
experience success. Although home visits are not necessarily a novel
idea, in my experience they provide both families and staff an avenue
for communication and hope—hope that together you can provide
a positive environment where their student feels valued and safe at
school.

Throughout the school year, have your mentors follow up with
the students on a regular basis, check in to see how their experience is
going, and work to get them connected to a school activity. They can
also monitor grades, contact their family to offer support, and share
reminders about attending important school events.

Hold breakfast and luncheons for the students and their families. Conduct surveys with the students, collect both quantitative
and qualitative data, and share those results with your staff and your
school board. By having students, parents, and staff talk about the
impact these experiences have had on the students and their overall
feelings about school, you will find out that others will want to support the program both monetarily and by becoming a mentor themselves. The personal connections you make will give you hope that

you can make a positive difference in the lives of young students by simply reaching out to them and their families and getting to know them on a more personal level.

CULTURE BUILDER #3

Teacher Calls—Take a day to call the parent(s) of your teachers and say thank you! Inspired by ideas I took from friends and colleagues Jeff Zoul (@Jeff_Zoul) and Dr. Sue Alborn-Yilek (@dr_sue_ay), I came up with a blended idea and decided to take action and follow up. I have always wanted to do something special for our staff members beyond the typical social gathering, personal note, etc. So one Saturday, I took the afternoon and made eleven phone calls, and when I was done, I kicked myself for not having done this in past years. I cannot even begin to describe the emotion, pride, and joy both the parents and I felt during our conversations. What I thought would be a short hello, thank you, and good-bye, turned into a discussion where I learned more about my teachers in one afternoon than I had during the course of the interview process, in-service, on-boarding, etc. I must admit I enjoyed the initial hesitation I could hear in their voices (I'm sure they were wondering, *Why is the principal calling me?*) That hesitation faded quickly when I told them how fortunate our school was to have their grown children teach our students. I was overcome by tears as I listened to these parents get emotional over the phone upon hearing my comments on the impact their children were having on our teachers and how it was directly attributed to the way in which they had raised their children. It was truly one of the greatest feelings I had felt as a principal, surpassed only by the feeling of watching students experience a sense of accomplishment after years of struggling to feel good about themselves.

"This is the most wonderful phone call I have ever received."

"I can't believe I got a call from my daughter's principal. You are so thoughtful. Thank you!"

"Our son has told us many great things about you, and he is so happy to be at Bettendorf!"

"I am just blown away! God bless you!"

When students or their colleagues begin to struggle, they serve as a merchant of hope by becoming a support system to pick up the pieces, lifting up their students and their colleagues with an encouraging kind word to help them refocus in a positive way. They take time to find the joy in their daily work while recognizing there will be challenges along the way, knowing every rose has its thorns. They see every thorn, however, as an opportunity for personal reflection because they know how they respond is their choice. This gives them a renewed sense of purpose because they can look past themselves and see that the most important gift is about serving others. In school communities that have been "culturalized," the staff accepts that they are only as good as their last decision and that they will not always get it right. Rather than make excuses when they fail, they accept it, apologize, and ask for forgiveness. They don't let failure define them, understanding that their opportunity to strive for excellence starts over right away. Through it all, they can manage the stress and the emotional toll with the support of their colleagues and keep going. They know in the end there is an abundance of joy waiting for them along with stories of success. That is what makes them stay: the opportunity to live their story and be a merchant of hope for those who have lost their way.

Being a merchant of hope is the fourth and final component of culturizing a school. It is everyone's duty, including yours, to foster a culture of hope, trust, and personal investment—one where each member of the school community feels as though he or she can accomplish anything together. Your students, parents, and colleagues need you to make those personal connections in order to better understand their stories, value their experiences, and cherish their struggles and their successes so they can continue to believe they, too, can make the collective impact they have always aspired to make.

QUESTIONS FOR DISCUSSION

» How do you/can we create experiences for students, teachers, and families that focus on supporting one another with kindness?

» When meeting with students and/or staff, what are some ways we can show them that we value them and care about them so, when they leave us, they feel motivated and inspired?

» What are some traditions you currently practice in your school community that honor the work of your students and staff? What are some practices that need to be added, re-examined, adjusted, or eliminated altogether?

» If you knew then what you know now about culturizing a school toward excellence, what is the first change you would make in your school—and why?

CHAPTER 6
It's Your Choice

Never lose sight of the fact that the most important measure of your success will be how you treat other people.

—Scott Eddy

I Wish I Knew Then What I Know Now

Being an educator has been one of the greatest joys of my life. There are still days I reflect on my journey and just shake my head in disbelief. I never take for granted what I do for a living, and I am genuinely grateful for the opportunities I have been given to make an impact on members of my profession. A dear friend and colleague of mine gave me this advice in my early twenties while I was quickly advancing my way up the administrative ladder.

She said, "Remember to spend less time focusing on your own accomplishments and focus more time on serving others so they, too, can experience their own successes. Only then will you experience the sense of accomplishment you hope to achieve." I have never forgotten those words.

During a trip to the 2016 NASSP (National Association for Secondary School Principals) Ignite conference, a gentleman reached out to me and asked me this question: "What do you wish you had known on your first day on the job as principal?" I responded by saying that I never realized the emotional toll that this job can take on any one individual. I simply wasn't prepared for that part of the job. I still believe this to be true, but this gentleman's question caused me to reflect even more, and the quote above made me wish I had taken more time to process his question and reflect on my answer. In hindsight, I wish someone had told me to....

Focus more on experiences—as I reflect on the past twenty-five years, I realize that, above all, experiences are what I cherish the most. The relationships we foster over time will ultimately dictate our happiness and our impact on others.

Take time to invest in myself as much as in others—as someone who was raised by parents who always served others first, I learned that lesson well. More recently, I have learned that I need to invest in myself as well. By doing so, I have seen the impact I can have on others is greater when I am in a better place. Sometimes we need to take time to fill our own cup.

Stay connected—the job of a school leader can be all consuming. By re-connecting to mentors, former co-workers, and current colleagues, you will gain a greater appreciation for the work that you are doing and recognize how much you have grown over time. The energy you gain from this perspective will launch you further down the right path.

Don't just tell them; show them—one pitfall for teachers and leaders is we want to tell people how to do things. If you want to influence change, don't tell others what it will look like; show them what it looks like. The visual impact to this strategy can be a game changer whether you are teaching a lesson to students or moving an organization forward.

Don't depend on the same teacher and leaders—every organization has a group of people who have a desire for more leadership roles. Be grateful that you have a core group from which to begin building capacity, but you cannot increase your capacity if you depend on the same people over and over to support your mission/vision. Give others the same opportunities by trusting in their abilities and showing your confidence in them to maximize their potential as leaders. And don't forget to utilize the voices and talents of your students to help lead your classroom or school forward.

Don't let the process become the product when trying to influence change. This can be frustrating, especially for your best people who have invested in you, the process, or a program. Think of it in this manner. Ensure that the process is democratic, but once the decision has been made and consensus has been reached, then the implementation must become autocratic in order to continue moving forward.

Stop putting so much emphasis on trying to be successful; instead, try spending more time on trying to leave your mark by being significant in the lives of others. This will leave you much more fulfilled.

Differentiate for staff like we do for students—this is especially true when it comes to professional development, evaluations, feedback, and/or growth plans. As a profession, we continue to expect all staff to meet the same standards at the same level at the same time. We must move toward a growth model of continuous improvement where failure is supported and reflection is required. Only through reflection and honest, genuine dialogue can we ever improve our craft. Everyone can benefit from a leadership coach.

If you want to improve your relationships with others, try changing the manner in which you have those conversations. Managing difficult people requires you to manage yourself first.

Focus on skill sets rather than knowledge when hiring staff—I need staff with the skills to use their knowledge in practical ways to lead, model, collaborate, and provoke greater learning, not only with their students but among their peers as well. By having the ability to apply what they learn, they can build confidence in themselves as well as others.

There are two ways to get in the last word—apologize and accept an apology.

Take responsibility for my own professional growth—I have come to accept that my experiences will be whatever I want them to be. One of my most satisfying and rewarding findings as principal was when I finally recognized that the only barrier to my own learning was my own unwillingness to learn.

Believe my words and my actions can inspire others—I have learned over the years that we can move others to want to be greater tomorrow than they are today, both through our words and our actions. It's about having a vision and then carrying that vision out with the support of others. In turn, this develops a culture of hope and faith that things can and will be better. We all have something to offer others from which they can learn. Believe you can make an impact.

I know there are others in my profession who do not feel the way I feel, and at times I have been criticized for seeing things through rose colored glasses. But I choose not to be like those who are unhappy or others who look weary and tired. That sounds too much like a job to me. I did not become an educator so I could become negative, bitter, or even cynical. I am not willing to accept that "things can never change" or feel that "I can only do so much." I have encountered principals, secretaries, teachers, district administrators, support staff, and teacher librarians who harbored such feelings. No one is immune. Rather than judge, I choose to believe that these folks were not always this way, and for reasons unbeknownst to all of us, somewhere in their own journey they simply lost their way. I believe great leaders can inspire them back to greatness.

After all these years, what do I still wish for? I wish to be able to help guide back those who have lost their way so they can experience their own successes. I want them to be able to feel the same sense of accomplishment I feel daily, if they can just remember that their experiences will be whatever they want them to be. With that said, choose wisely.

All classroom teachers and school leaders should have a fundamental core belief system from which to draw if they want to ensure high expectations, fairness, and equity for all students and staff. Whether you are leading a school, teaching reading to third graders, leading rehearsals for the school orchestra, working in the school attendance office, assisting a student one-on-one as a paraprofessional, or serving as a school counselor, every individual should be deriving their philosophy and responding to the needs of others from a fundamental core set of principles. By doing so, both students and staff alike will maintain a strong understanding of what is expected of them, and this will then begin to define the very culture in which they serve.

If our ultimate desire is to cultivate cultures of excellence where people feel secure in striving for greatness, then we must learn to navigate around the status quo. Our desire should never settle in simply making an impact; we should strive to make the greatest impact we possibly can. This cannot be achieved if we allow average to become our standard. Why is it then that so many cultures succumb to average? It is because school leaders fail to acknowledge and address *awfulizers* who do everything in their negative power to suck the life out of the best people in the organization. It is therefore imperative that school leaders support the best by expecting the best, recognizing that their team won't always be able to give them one hundred percent every day due to external factors beyond their control. How can we expect staff to give one hundred percent when they are serving as a caretaker for an elderly parent? Just as challenging are those times when our school family whom we care deeply about are suffering in their relationships, facing a potential breakup, separation, or even divorce. Or how about when a colleague comes to you and confides in you that her twelve-year-old daughter refused to go to school that morning and shared with her that she no longer wanted to live and was dealing with thoughts of suicide? These are life changing situations from which no staff member in any school is immune, yet it affects the performance level of even our most gifted and talented teachers. We cannot let failure define the work we do. We must also take ownership for our missteps and then work to correct them, recognizing that our personal excellence starts over every day. We must therefore continue to combat average by identifying excellence in our organizations and then surrounding it with more excellence. How do excellent teachers and leaders behave?

They....

- **Model the behaviors they want to see repeated.** They smile a lot, engage everyone they see in genuine conversation, clean up a mess rather than call a custodian to clean it up, apologize to a student or staff member and ask for forgiveness, say "we" and "our" instead of "I" and "my" when sharing success stories. They intentionally seek out those in their schools who go above and beyond and tell them how much they appreciate them.

- **Don't dwell on problems, but rather cherish the conversations.** They see every challenge as an opportunity to initiate a conversation that, if done appropriately, will lead to more conversations and cultivate a more positive and meaningful relationship that did not exist previously.

- **Look past the workload.** The work is never going away, so they begin to embrace the value in the work they do and share the positives with others that come from it with a sense of passion, purpose, and pride rather than complain about it. They have learned that complaining about it says more about them than the work they are paid to do.

- **Gather energy from others with whom they interact.** They focus on serving and fulfilling the needs of others, inherently knowing they will feel good about the work they do and derive more energy from it. They then repeat this process over and over.

- **Foster a sense of pride in the building everywhere.** They pay close attention to even the smallest of details. Teachers recognize the importance of learning spaces and redesign their classroom space with assistance from their students to make it a place that inspires them to want to learn. Principals walk the school building and grounds at least once a week and take notes on where items need to be addressed. They view every irregularity as a coffee stain on a shirt or blouse that needs to be washed or dry-cleaned right away. They work alongside their custodial and grounds crew teams to model the standard they expect and then make sure they take time to recognize the changes and celebrate them together.

- **Don't allow others to opt out of doing.** When administrators, teachers, para-professionals, etc., opt out of what is communicated or is expected to be done, that is not a staff issue; it's a leadership issue. The same holds true for teachers in many instances when student discipline issues become the norm. Often upon further investigation, we find it is not a student issue but rather an adult/ teacher issue. They eliminate opting out and hold people accountable. They bring their best to every situation and expect others to do the same. They desire to be the standard by which others in their organization are measured.

- **Take time to think and then follow up with action.** Sometimes it is necessary to take more time to process information when making decisions. They don't fall victim, however, to staying in processing mode for fear of making a decision. Thinking is necessary, but so is doing. They have the courage to act and make something happen, recognizing that by not making a decision they have, in fact, made a decision, thus losing the confidence and faith of their team regarding their leadership skills.

- **Don't wait for others to change.** They change. They take responsibility for their own behavior. They choose not to paralyze themselves because others are not doing the things that need to be done. They take initiative to be the change, not the same.

- **Never stop learning from others.** There is no shame in admitting that they don't know how to do something. They are not disingenuous and don't fake their way through something when they could have gained more credibility by simply admitting that they did not know something. They model learning first, second, and always.

- **Find the right balance in the "what ifs."** They rarely make decisions based on "What if this happens?" because they don't want to lose out on ninety-five percent of the great things that won't happen if they're focused on the five percent of the "what ifs." They also want their students and staff to live in a "what if" world that focuses on the part that asks, "What if we went for it? What if we did this instead? What if we contacted so and so and did such and such?" They recognize that it is in this world where the dreamers and disruptors live and allow themselves and others to dare to be different and then to go for it.

- **Inspire people and their ideas.** When a student, colleague, or staff member approaches them with an idea they are clearly excited about, their charge is to make sure that, when that person leaves, they are more excited about their idea than they were before they met with them. They do this by offering words of encouragement and telling them they appreciate their willingness to push their thinking to new heights. They ask specific questions that support their idea, and they follow up and comment about how they have been thinking about their idea and offer fresh ideas that align with their initial thoughts. In other words, they lift their people and their ideas up; they don't push them down or dismiss them. They know the key to sustainable positive change in any environment is to trust their people so that their people trust them.

We cannot allow ourselves to live in a world that accepts status quo as our standard. We are so much better than that, and our kids and our employees deserve more than just average. In fact, by accepting average we run the risk of eventually falling back to *below* average. Without question, every now and then, we will find ourselves visiting the world of average, but when that happens, let's not take up residence. Let us rather act with a sense of urgency to re-culturize our schools, acknowledging there is no room for the status quo.

What an incredible time it is to be an educator! Begin today to cultivate a culture of excellence where staff members are confident in their decisions, feel comfortable living in a culture of yes, and don't fear having to keep their head down and having to stay in their lane due to a toxic culture. Be mindful of the fact that we cannot build a community of leaders if our team has to seek permission each time before making a decision.

It is in these moments confronting the status quo that we must rise above and make our impact by visualizing a culture of excellence through the eyes of the school community, not merely our own eyes. Seize the opportunity to culturize a community of leaders who are driven by a greater purpose to be the change that our students and staff so desperately seek and deserve. Our schools will be what they are because of the work you do.

As Mahatma Ghandi so eloquently stated, "Be the change you wish to see in the world."

Lead with passion.

Live with purpose.

Love with pride.

It's your choice how you want to live each day!

I encourage you to live your life so when others think of excellence, they think of you. In the end, your legacy won't be about your success; it will be about your significance and the impact you made on every student, every day, and whether you were willing to do whatever it took to inspire them to be more than they ever thought possible.

THANK YOU

To my family: For never giving up on me and loving me unconditionally. Through the long hours, late nights, missed dinners, and family nights, you sacrificed so much so I could be the best teacher and leader possible.

To my office team: You raised the bar for me, and you made coming to work enjoyable. More importantly, you filled me with love, empathy, and energy. You instilled in me a confidence that we could be the change our students and staff deserved.

To my editor, cover designer, and publisher: You showed me the way and then stood by me to help me find my voice, my confidence, and a belief in myself that anything is possible when I surround myself with excellence!

WORKS CITED

Wormeli, Rick. *Fair Isn't Always Equal: Assessing and Grading in the Differentiated Classroom.* Portland, ME: Stenhouse Publishers, 2006.

Meyer, Urban, and Wayne R. Coffey. *Above the Line: Lessons in Leadership and Life from a Championship Season.* New York : Penguin Press, 2015.

Schon, D. "Leadership-Life Fit." Presentation: Elementary Principals Statewide Mentoring Meeting, 2012.

Pierson, Rita. "Every Kid Needs a Champion." Filmed May 2013 at TED Talks for Education, video 7:45, ted.com/talks/ rita_pierson_every_kid_needs_a_champion.

Sinanis, Tony, and Joseph Sanfelippo. *The power of branding: telling your school's story.* Thousand Oaks, CA: Corwin, 2015.

Goldman, Robert and Stephen Papson, *Nike Culture: The Sign of the Swoosh.* London: Sage Publications, 1998.

More From

Teach Like a PIRATE

Increase Student Engagement, Boost Your Creativity, and Transform Your Life as an Educator
By Dave Burgess (@BurgessDave)

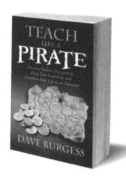

    Teach Like a PIRATE is the New York Times' best-selling book that has sparked a worldwide educational revolution. It is part inspirational manifesto that ignites passion for the profession and part practical road map, filled with dynamic strategies to dramatically increase student engagement. Translated into multiple languages, its message resonates with educators who want to design outrageously creative lessons and transform school into a life-changing experience for students.

Learn Like a PIRATE

Empower Your Students to Collaborate, Lead, and Succeed

By Paul Solarz (@PaulSolarz)

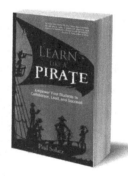

    Today's job market demands that students be prepared to take responsibility for their lives and careers. We do them a disservice if we teach them how to earn passing grades without equipping them to take charge of their education. In *Learn Like a PIRATE*, Paul Solarz explains how to design classroom experiences that encourage students to take risks and explore their passions in a stimulating, motivating, and supportive environment where improvement, rather than grades, is the focus. Discover how student-led classrooms help students thrive and develop into self-directed, confident citizens who are capable of making smart, responsible decisions, all on their own.

P is for PIRATE

Inspirational ABC's for Educators

By Dave and Shelley Burgess (@Burgess_Shelley)

Teaching is an adventure that stretches the imagination and calls for creativity every day! In *P is for PIRATE*, husband and wife team Dave and Shelley Burgess encourage and inspire educators to make their classrooms fun and exciting places to learn. Tapping into years of personal experience and drawing on the insights of more than seventy educators, the authors offer a wealth of ideas for making learning and teaching more fulfilling than ever before.

Play Like a Pirate

Engage Students with Toys, Games, and Comics. Make Your Classroom Fun Again!

By Quinn Rollins (@jedikermit)

Yes! School can be simultaneously fun and educational. In *Play Like a Pirate*, Quinn Rollins offers practical, engaging strategies and resources that make it easy to integrate fun into your curriculum. Regardless of the grade level you teach, you'll find inspiration and ideas that will help you engage your students in unforgettable ways.

eXPlore Like a Pirate

Gamification and Game-Inspired Course Design to Engage, Enrich, and Elevate Your Learners

By Michael Matera (@MrMatera)

Are you ready to transform your classroom into an experiential world that flourishes on collaboration and creativity? Then set sail with classroom game designer and educator Michael Matera as he reveals the possibilities and power of game-based learning. In *eXPlore Like a Pirate*, Matera serves as your experienced guide to help you apply the most motivational techniques of gameplay to your classroom. You'll learn gamification strategies that will work with and enhance (rather than replace) your current curriculum and discover how these engaging methods can be applied to any grade level or subject.

The Innovator's Mindset

Empower Learning, Unleash Talent,
and Lead a Culture of Creativity

By George Couros (@gcouros)

The traditional system of education requires students to hold their questions and compliantly stick to the scheduled curriculum. But our job as educators is to provide new and better opportunities for our students. It's time to recognize that compliance doesn't foster innovation, encourage critical thinking, or inspire creativity—and those are the skills our students need to succeed. In *The Innovator's Mindset*, George Couros encourages teachers and administrators to empower their learners to wonder, to explore—and to become forward-thinking leaders.

Master the Media

How Teaching Media Literacy Can
Save Our Plugged-in World

By Julie Smith (@julnilsmith)

Written to help teachers and parents educate the next generation, *Master the Media* explains the history, purpose, and messages behind the media. The point isn't to get kids to unplug; it's to help them make informed choices, understand the difference between truth and lies, and discern perception from reality. Critical thinking leads to smarter decisions—and it's why media literacy can save the world.

The Zen Teacher

Creating FOCUS, SIMPLICITY, and
TRANQUILITY in the Classroom

By Dan Tricarico (@TheZenTeacher)

Teachers have incredible power to influence—even improve—the future. In *The Zen Teacher*, educator, blogger, and speaker Dan Tricarico provides practical, easy-to-use techniques to help teachers be their best—unrushed and fully focused—so they can maximize their performance and improve their quality of life. In this introductory guide, Dan Tricarico explains what it means to develop a Zen practice—something that has nothing to do with religion and everything to do with your ability to thrive in the classroom.

Lead Like a PIRATE

Make School Amazing for Your Students and Staff

By Shelley Burgess and Beth Houf
(@Burgess_Shelley, @BethHouf)

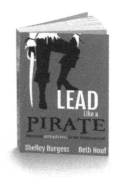

In *Lead Like a PIRATE*, education leaders Shelley Burgess and Beth Houf map out the character traits necessary to captain a school or district. You'll learn where to find the treasure that's already in your classrooms and schools—and how to bring out the very best in your educators. This book will equip and encourage you to be relentless in your quest to make school amazing for your students, staff, parents, and communities.

50 Things You Can Do with Google Classroom

By Alice Keeler and Libbi Miller
(@AliceKeeler, @MillerLibbi)

It can be challenging to add new technology to the classroom, but it's a must if students are going to be well-equipped for the future. Alice Keeler and Libbi Miller shorten the learning curve by providing a thorough overview of the Google Classroom App. Part of Google Apps for Education (GAfE), Google Classroom was specifically designed to help teachers save time by streamlining the process of going digital. Complete with screenshots, *50 Things You Can Do with Google Classroom* provides ideas and step-by-step instructions to help teachers implement this powerful tool.

50 Things to Go Further with Google Classroom

A Student-Centered Approach

By Alice Keeler and Libbi Miller
(@AliceKeeler, @MillerLibbi)

Today's technology empowers educators to move away from the traditional classroom where teachers lead and students work independently—each doing the same thing. In *50 Things to Go Further with Google Classroom: A Student-Centered Approach*, authors and educators Alice Keeler and Libbi Miller offer inspiration and resources to help you create a digitally rich, engaging, student-centered environment. They show you how to tap into the power of individualized learning that is possible with Google Classroom.

Pure Genius

Building a Culture of Innovation and
Taking 20% Time to the Next Level

By Don Wettrick (@DonWettrick)

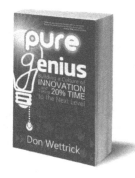

For far too long, schools have been bastions of boredom, killers of creativity, and way too comfortable with compliance and conformity. In *Pure Genius*, Don Wettrick explains how collaboration—with experts, students, and other educators—can help you create interesting, and even life-changing, opportunities for learning. Wettrick's book inspires and equips educators with a systematic blueprint for teaching innovation in any school.

140 Twitter Tips for Educators

Get Connected, Grow Your Professional
Learning Network, and Reinvigorate Your Career

By Brad Currie, Billy Krakower, and Scott Rocco
(@bradmcurrie, @wkrakower, @ScottRRocco)

Whatever questions you have about education or about how you can be even better at your job, you'll find ideas, resources, and a vibrant network of professionals ready to help you on Twitter. In *140 Twitter Tips for Educators*, #Satchat hosts and founders of Evolving Educators, Brad Currie, Billy Krakower, and Scott Rocco, offer step-by-step instructions to help you master the basics of Twitter, build an online following, and become a Twitter rock star.

Ditch That Textbook

Free Your Teaching and Revolutionize
Your Classroom

By Matt Miller (@jmattmiller)

Textbooks are symbols of centuries-old education. They're often outdated as soon as they hit students' desks. Acting "by the textbook" implies compliance and a lack of creativity. It's time to ditch those textbooks—and those textbook assumptions about learning! In *Ditch That Textbook*, teacher and blogger Matt Miller encourages educators to throw out meaningless, pedestrian teaching and learning practices. He empowers them to evolve and improve on old, standard teaching methods. *Ditch That Textbook* is a support system, toolbox, and manifesto to help educators free their teaching and revolutionize their classrooms.

How Much Water Do We Have?

5 Success Principles for Conquering Any
Challenge and Thriving in Times of Change

by Pete Nunweiler with Kris Nunweiler

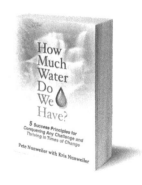

In *How Much Water Do We Have?* Pete Nunweiler identifies five key elements—information, planning, motivation, support, and leadership—that are necessary for the success of any goal, life transition, or challenge. Referring to these elements as the 5 Waters of Success, Pete explains that, like the water we drink, you need them to thrive in today's rapidly paced world. If you're feeling stressed out, overwhelmed, or uncertain at work or at home, pause and look for the signs of dehydration. Learn how to find, acquire, and use the 5 Waters of Success—so you can share them with your team and family members.

Instant Relevance

Using Today's Experiences to Teach Tomorrow's Lessons

By Denis Sheeran (@MathDenisNJ)

Every day, students in schools around the world ask the question, "When am I ever going to use this in real life?" In *Instant Relevance*, author and keynote speaker Denis Sheeran equips you to create engaging lessons *from* experiences and events that matter to your students. Learn how to help your students see meaningful connections between the real world and what they learn in the classroom—because that's when learning sticks.

The Classroom Chef

Sharpen Your Lessons. Season Your Classes.
Make Math Meaningful.

By John Stevens and Matt Vaudrey
(@Jstevens009, @MrVaudrey)

In *The Classroom Chef*, math teachers and instructional coaches John Stevens and Matt Vaudrey share their secret recipes, ingredients, and tips for serving up lessons that engage students and help them "get" math. You can use these ideas and methods as-is, or better yet, tweak them and create your own enticing educational meals. The message the authors share is that, with imagination and preparation, every teacher can be a classroom chef.

Start. Right. Now.

Teach and Lead for Excellence

By Todd Whitaker, Jeff Zoul, and Jimmy Casas
(@ToddWhitaker, @Jeff_Zoul, @casas_jimmy)

In their work leading up to *Start. Right. Now.*, Todd Whitaker, Jeff Zoul, and Jimmy Casas studied educators from across the nation and discovered four key behaviors of excellence: Excellent leaders and teachers *Know the Way, Show the Way, Go the Way, and Grow Each Day*. If you are ready to take the first step toward excellence, this motivating book will put you on the right path.

The Writing on the Classroom Wall

How Posting Your Most Passionate Beliefs about Education Can Empower Your Students, Propel Your Growth, and Lead to a Lifetime of Learning

By Steve Wyborney (@SteveWyborney)

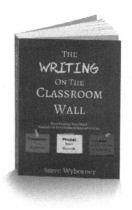

In *The Writing on the Classroom Wall*, Steve Wyborney explains how posting and discussing Big Ideas can lead to deeper learning. You'll learn why sharing your ideas will sharpen and refine them. You'll also be encouraged to know that the Big Ideas you share don't have to be profound to make a profound impact on learning. In fact, Steve explains, it's okay if some of your ideas fall *off* the wall. What matters most is sharing them.

LAUNCH

Using Design Thinking to Boost Creativity and Bring Out the Maker in Every Student

By John Spencer and A.J. Juliani
(@spencerideas, @ajjuliani)

Something happens in students when they define themselves as *makers* and *inventors* and *creators*. They discover powerful skills—problem-solving, critical thinking, and imagination—that will help them shape the world's future ... *our* future. In *LAUNCH*, John Spencer and A.J. Juliani provide a process that can be incorporated into every class at every grade level ... even if you don't consider yourself a "creative teacher." And if you dare to innovate and view creativity as an essential skill, you will empower your students to change the world—starting right now.

Kids Deserve It!

Pushing Boundaries and Challenging
Conventional Thinking

By Todd Nesloney and Adam Welcome
(@TechNinjaTodd, @awelcome)

In *Kids Deserve It!*, Todd and Adam encourage you to think big and make learning fun and meaningful for students. Their high-tech, high-touch, and highly engaging practices will inspire you to take risks, shake up the status quo, and be a champion for your students. While you're at it, you just might rediscover why you became an educator in the first place.

Escaping the School Leader's Dunk Tank

How to Prevail When Others Want to See You Drown

By Rebecca Coda and Rick Jetter
(@RebeccaCoda, @RickJetter)

No school leader is immune to the effects of discrimination, bad politics, revenge, or ego-driven coworkers. These kinds of dunk-tank situations can make an educator's life miserable. By sharing real-life stories and insightful research, the authors (who are dunk-tank survivors themselves) equip school leaders with the practical knowledge and emotional tools necessary to survive and, better yet, avoid getting "dunked."

Your School Rocks...So Tell People!

Passionately Pitch and Promote the
Positives Happening on Your Campus

By Ryan McLane and Eric Lowe
(@McLane_Ryan, @EricLowe21)

Great things are happening in your school every day. The problem is, no one beyond your school walls knows about them. School principals Ryan McLane and Eric Lowe want to help you get the word out! In *Your School Rocks ... So Tell People!*, McLane and Lowe offer more than seventy immediately actionable tips along with easy-to-follow instructions and links to video tutorials. This practical guide will equip you to create an effective and manageable communication strategy using social media tools. Learn how to keep your students' families and community connected, informed, and excited about what's going on in your school.

Teaching Math with Google Apps

50 G Suite Activities

By Alice Keeler and Diana Herrington
(@AliceKeeler, @mathdiana)

Google Apps give teachers the opportunity to interact with students in a more meaningful way than ever before, while G Suite empowers students to be creative, critical thinkers who collaborate as they explore and learn. In *Teaching Math with Google Apps*, educators Alice Keeler and Diana Herrington demonstrate fifty different ways to bring math classes to the twenty-first century with easy-to-use technology.

Table Talk Math

A Practical Guide for Bringing Math into Everyday Conversations

By John Stevens (@Jstevens009)

Making math part of families' everyday conversations is a powerful way to help children and teens learn to love math. In *Table Talk Math*, John Stevens offers parents (and teachers!) ideas for initiating authentic, math-based conversations that will get kids to notice and be curious about all the numbers, patterns, and equations in the world around them.

Shift This!

How to Implement Gradual Changes for MASSIVE Impact in Your Classroom

By Joy Kirr (@JoyKirr)

Establishing a student-led culture that isn't focused on grades and homework but on individual responsibility and personalized learning may seem like a daunting task—especially if you think you have to do it all at once. But significant change is possible, sustainable, and even easy when it happens little by little. In *Shift This!*, educator and speaker Joy Kirr explains how to make gradual shifts—in your thinking, teaching, and approach to classroom design—that will have a massive impact in your classroom. Make the first shift today!

Unmapped Potential

An Educator's Guide to Lasting Change

By Julie Hasson and Missy Lennard (@PPrincipals)

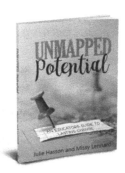

No matter where you are in your educational career, chances are you have, at times, felt overwhelmed and overworked. Maybe you feel that way right now. If so, you aren't alone. But the more important news is that things can get better! You simply need the right map to guide you from frustrated to fulfilled. *Unmapped Potential* offers advice and practical strategies to help you find your unique path to becoming the kind of educator—the kind of person—you want to be.

Social LEADia

Moving Students from Digital Citizenship to Digital Leadership

By Jennifer Casa-Todd (@JCasaTodd)

Equipping students for their future begins by helping them become digital leaders now. In our networked society, students need to learn how to leverage social media to connect to people, passions, and opportunities to grow and make a difference. *Social LEADia* addresses the need to shift the conversations at school and at home from digital citizenship to digital leadership.

Shattering the Perfect Teacher Myth

6 Truths That Will Help You THRIVE as an Educator

By Aaron Hogan (@aaron_hogan)

The idyllic myth of the perfect teacher perpetuates unrealistic expectations that erode self-confidence and set teachers up for failure. Author and educator Aaron Hogan is on a mission to shatter the myth of the perfect teacher by equipping educators with strategies that help them shift out of survival mode and THRIVE.

Spark Learning

3 Keys to Embracing the Power of Student Curiosity

By Ramsey Musallam (@ramusallam)

Inspired by his popular TED Talk "3 Rules to Spark Learning," this book combines brain science research, proven teaching methods, and Ramsey's personal story to empower you to improve your students' learning experiences by inspiring inquiry and harnessing its benefits. If you want to engage students in more interesting and effective learning, this is the book for you.

The Four O'Clock Faculty

A Rogue Guide to Revolutionizing Professional Development

By Rich Czyz (@RACzyz)

Author Rich Czyz is on a mission to revolutionize professional learning for all educators. In *The Four O'Clock Faculty*, Rich identifies ways to make PD meaningful, efficient, and, above all, personally relevant. This book is a practical guide that reveals why some PD is so awful and what you can do to change the model for the betterment of you and your colleagues.

Ditch That Homework

Practical Strategies to Help Make Homework Obsolete

By Matt Miller and Alice Keeler (@jmattmiller, @alicekeeler)

In *Ditch That Homework*, Matt Miller and Alice Keeler discuss the pros and cons of homework, why teachers assign it, and what life could look like without it. As they evaluate the research and share parent and teacher insights, the authors offer a convincing case for ditching homework and replacing it with more effective and personalized learning methods.

About the Author

Jimmy Casas has twenty-two years of school leadership experience at the secondary level. He received his BA in Spanish and master's in teaching from the University of Iowa and his master's in educational leadership from Cardinal Stritch University in Milwaukee. Jimmy earned his superintendent endorsement from Drake University, where he serves as an adjunct professor, teaching a graduate course on educational leadership. During his tenure as principal, his passion for teaching and learning, coupled with a vision for developing a community of leaders, procured a culture of excellence and high standards for learning amid a positive school culture for students and staff. Jimmy's core purpose lies in serving others. He continues to give back to his profession by speaking and presenting at the local, state, and national levels and school districts around the country. He was named the 2012 Iowa Secondary Principal of the Year and was selected as one of three finalists for NASSP 2013 National

Secondary Principal of the Year. In 2014, Jimmy was invited to the White House to speak on the Future Ready Schools pledge. In 2015, he was named the Bammy National Principal of the Year. Jimmy is the co-Founder of EdCampIowa and the co-Founder of #IAedchat, a popular on-line chat. Jimmy is the co-author of two other books with Todd Whitaker and Jeff Zoul entitled, *What Connected Educators Do Differently* and *Start. Right. Now.: Teach and Lead for Excellence.*

Jimmy currently serves as a Senior Fellow for the International Center for Leadership in Education (ICLE) and serves on the Professional Development Faculty for NASSP. Lastly, he is the co-founder and CEO of ConnectEDD, an educational leadership company aimed at organizing world-class professional learning conferences and professional development services across the country entitled What Great Educators Do Differently.